FOR ORGANS, PIANOS & ELECTRONIC KEYBOARDS

E-Z Play Today
175

PARTY SONGS

40 Tunes to Get Any Party Started

Including Fight for Your Right (To Party) • Get Down Tonight
Limbo Rock • My Sharona • Super Freak • Y.M.C.A.

T0081500

ISBN- 978-1-4234-2182-5

HAL•LEONARD®
CORPORATION
7777 W. BLUEMOUND RD. P.O. BOX 13819 MILWAUKEE, WI 53213

E-Z PLAY® TODAY Music Notation © 1975 by HAL LEONARD CORPORATION
E-Z PLAY and EASY ELECTRONIC KEYBOARD MUSIC are registered trademarks of HAL LEONARD CORPORATION.

Visit Hal Leonard Online at
www.halleonard.com

PARTY SONGS

The Chicken Dance

Registration 9
Rhythm: Polka

By Terry Rendall
and Werner Thomas

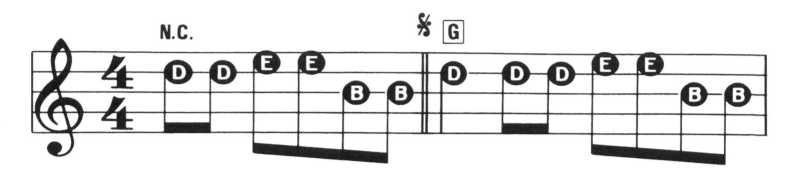

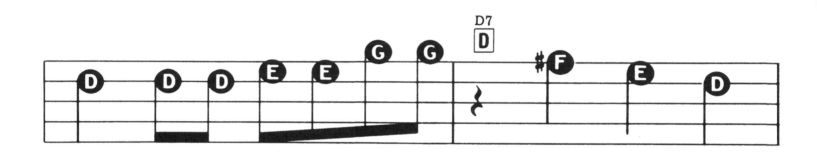

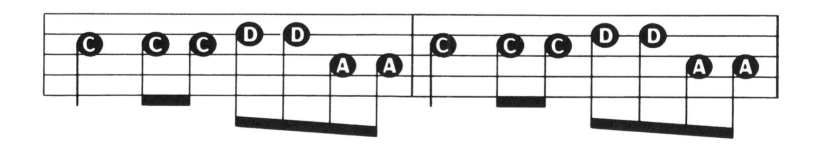

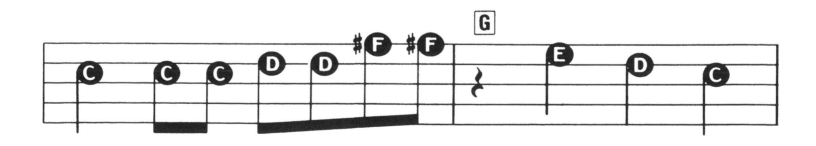

5

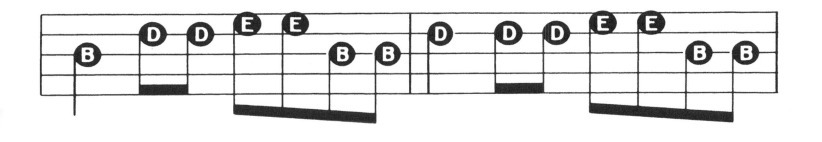

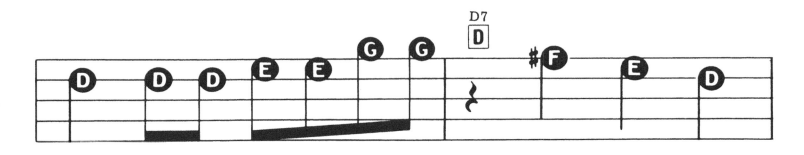

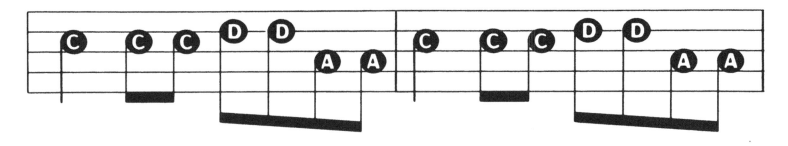

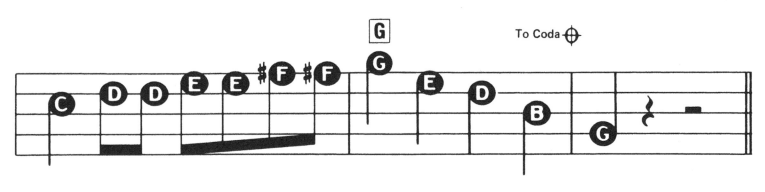

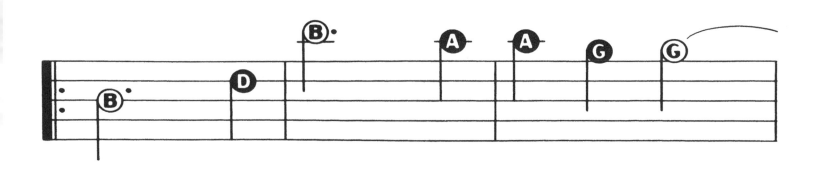

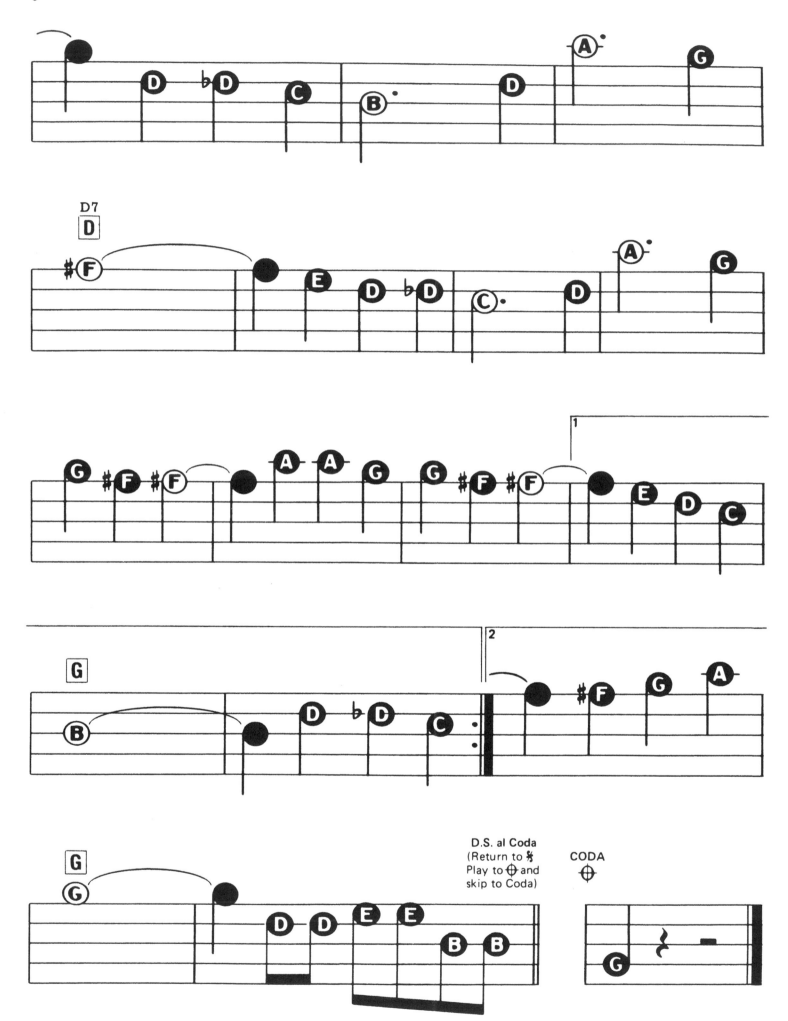

Copacabana
(At the Copa)

Registration 1
Rhythm: Disco

Music by Barry Manilow
Lyric by Bruce Sussman and Jack Feldman

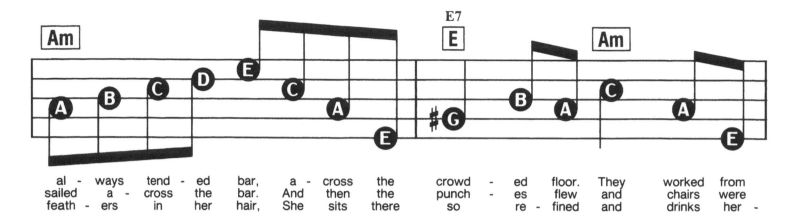

al - ways tend - ed bar, a - cross the crowd - ed floor. They worked from
sailed a - cross the bar. And then the punch - es flew and chairs were
feath - ers in her hair, She sits there so re - fined and drinks her -

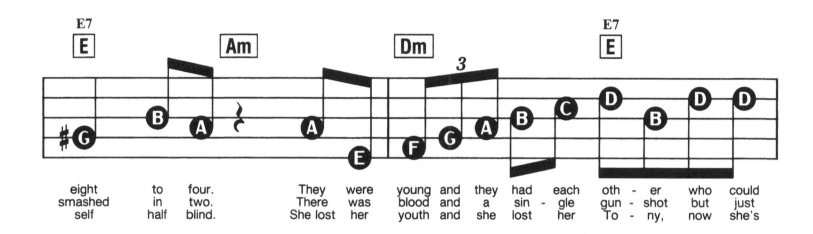

eight to four. They were young and they had each oth - er who could
smashed in two. There was young blood and a sin - gle gun - shot but could just
self half blind. She lost her youth and she lost her To - ny, now she's

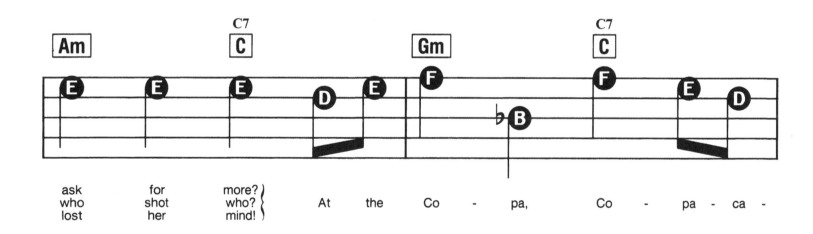

ask for more?⎫
who shot who?⎬ At the Co - pa, Co - pa - ca -
lost her mind!⎭

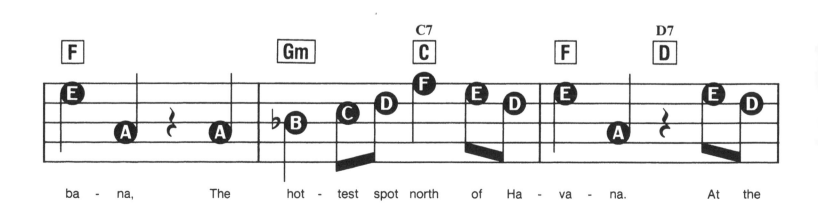

ba - na, The hot - test spot north of Ha - va - na. At the

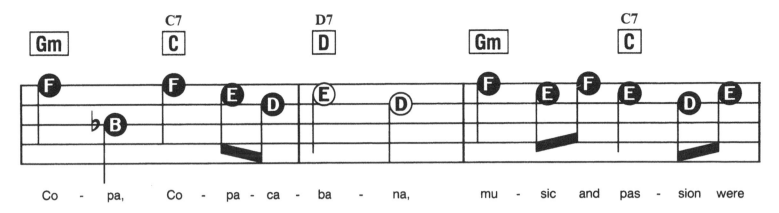

Co - pa, Co - pa - ca - ba - na, mu - sic and pas - sion were

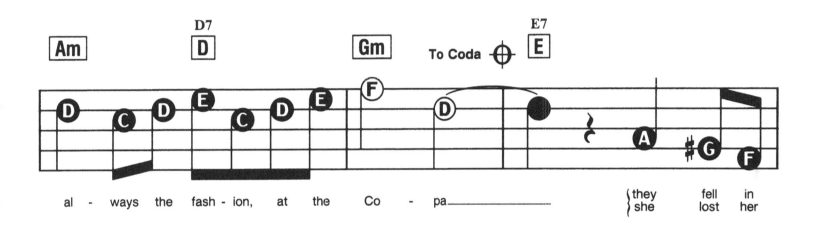

al - ways the fash - ion, at the Co - pa_____ {they fell in
{she lost her

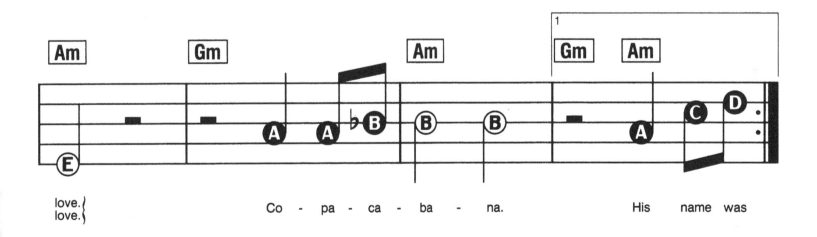

love.} Co - pa - ca - ba - na. His name was
love.{

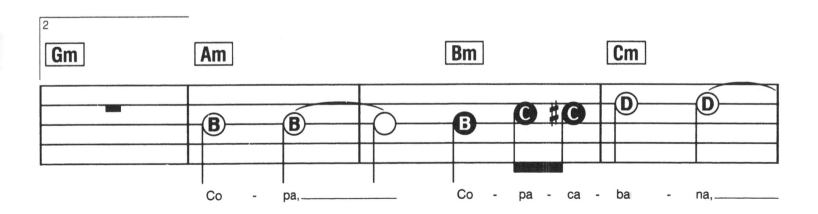

Co - pa,_____ Co - pa - ca - ba - na,_____

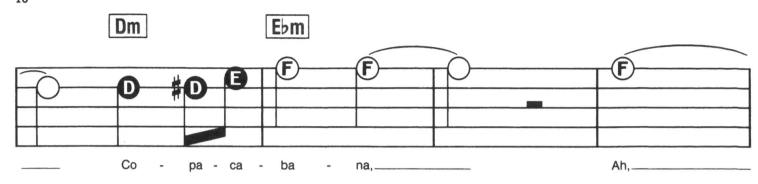

Co - pa - ca - ba - na,_____ Ah,_____

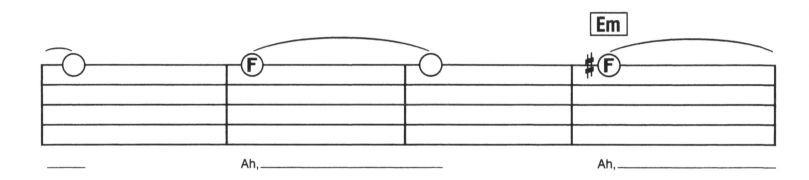

Ah,_____ Ah,_____

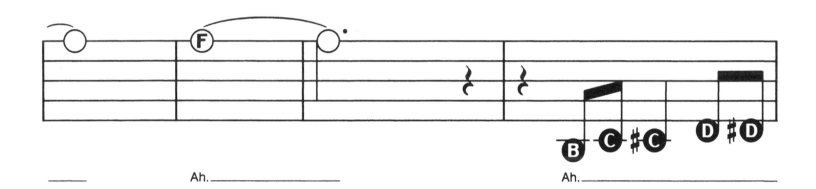

_____ Ah._____ Ah._____

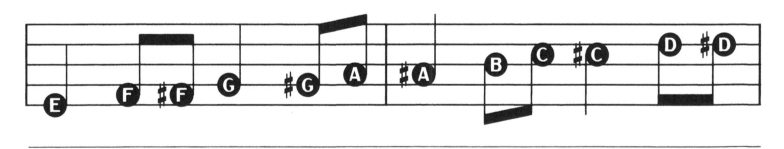

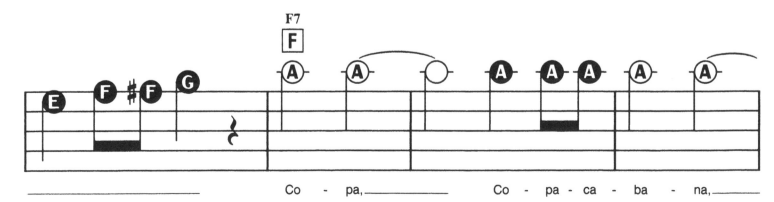

Co - pa,_____ Co - pa - ca - ba - na,_____

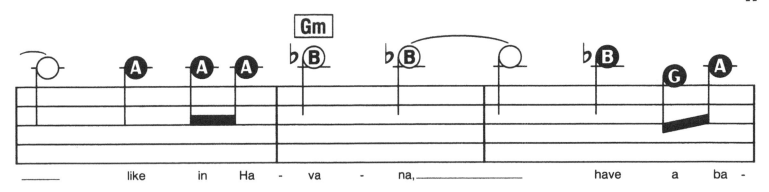

like in Ha - va - na, _____ have a ba -

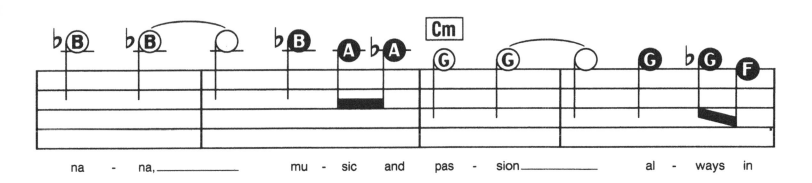

na - na, ____ mu - sic and pas - sion ____ al - ways in

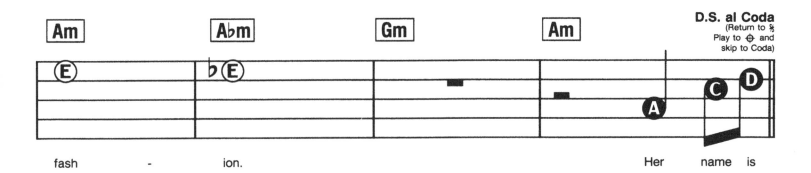

fash - ion. Her name is

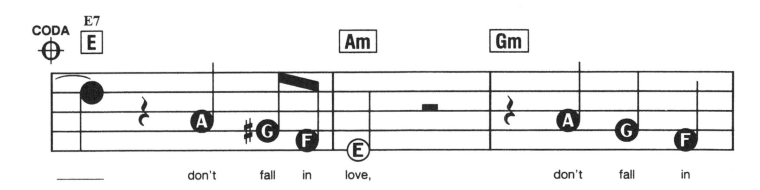

____ don't fall in love, don't fall in

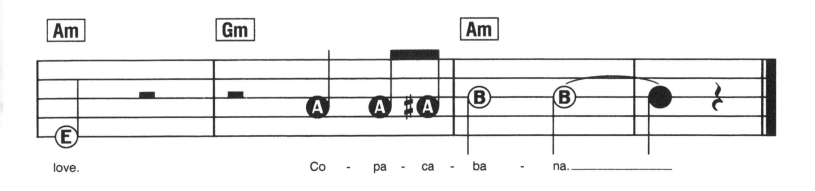

love. Co - pa - ca - ba - na. ____

Dancing Queen

Registration 2
Rhythm: Rock or 8 Beat

Words and Music by Benny Andersson,
Björn Ulvaeus and Stig Anderson

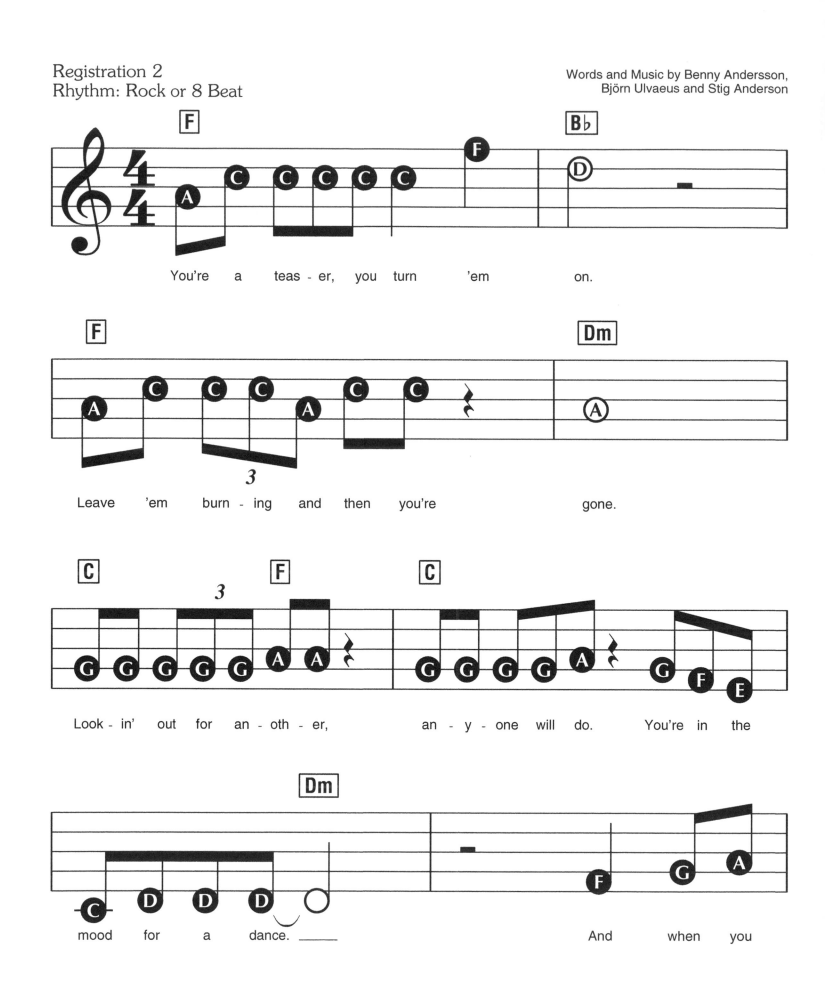

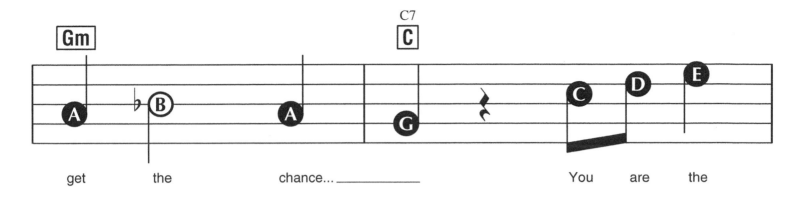

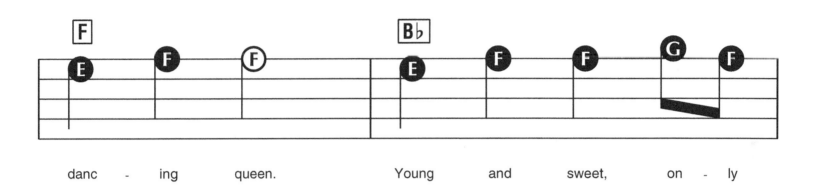

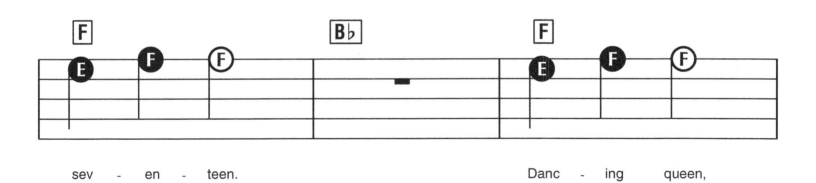

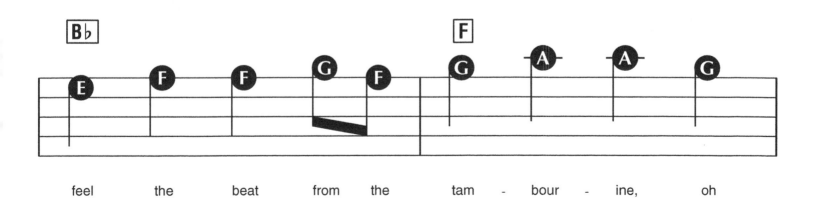

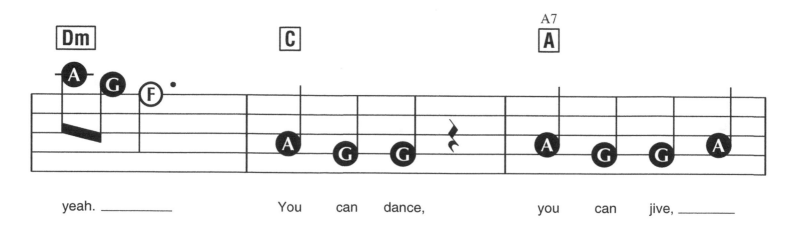

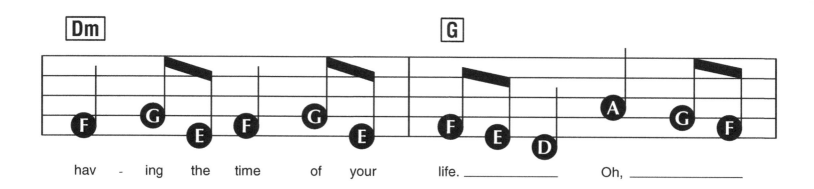

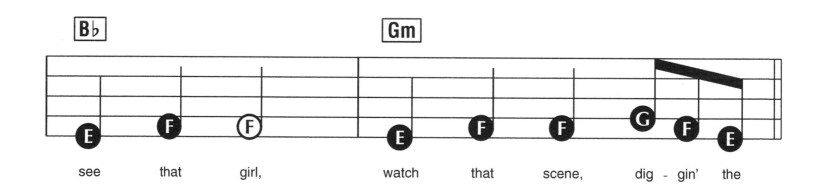

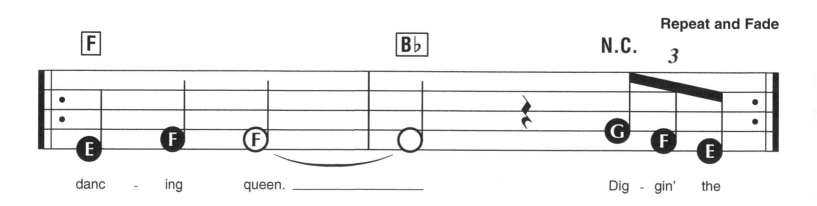

Electric Slide

Registration 4
Rhythm: 8 Beat or Rock

Words and Music by
Neville Livingston

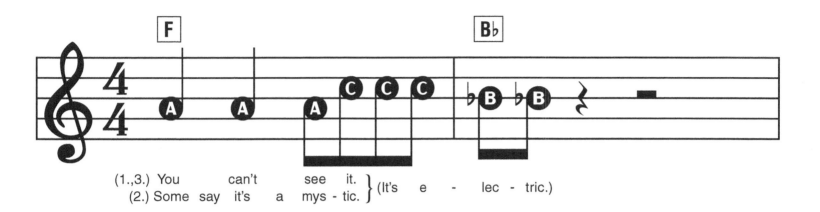

(1.,3.) You can't see it. } (It's e - lec - tric.)
(2.) Some say it's a mys - tic.

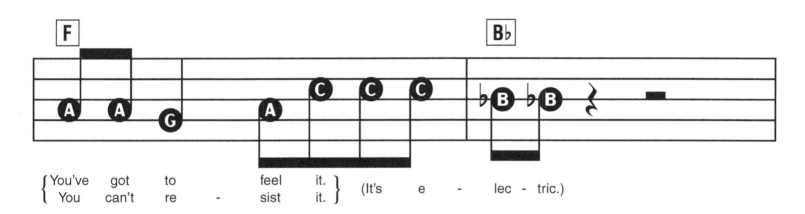

{ You've got to feel it. } (It's e - lec - tric.)
{ You can't re - sist it.

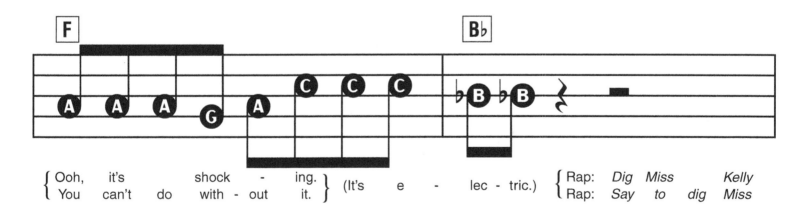

{ Ooh, it's shock - ing. } (It's e - lec - tric.)   { Rap: *Dig Miss Kelly*
{ You can't do with - out it.   { Rap: *Say to dig Miss*

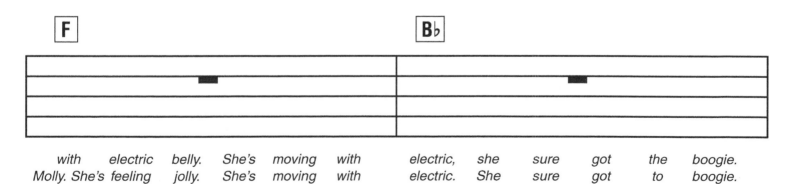

with electric belly. She's moving with electric, she sure got the boogie.
Molly. She's feeling jolly. She's moving with electric. She sure got to boogie.

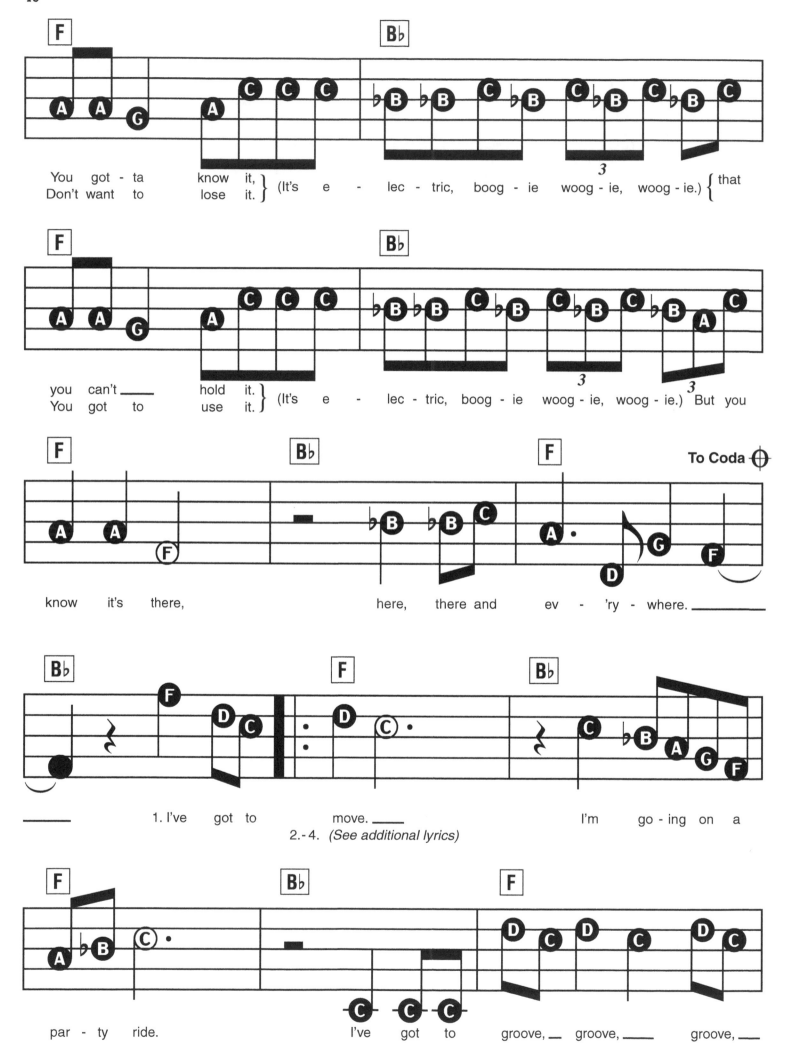

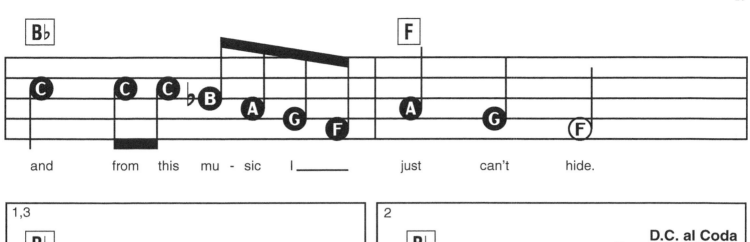

and   from this mu - sic I _____ just   can't   hide.

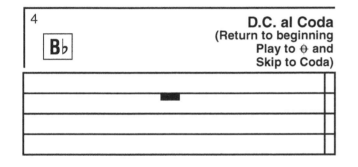

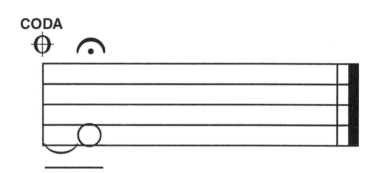

2. Are   you   com - ing
4. I've   got   to

CODA

Additional Lyrics

2. Are you coming with me?
   Come, let me take you on a party ride,
   And I'll teach you, teach you, teach you,
   I'll teach you the electric slide.

3. *Instrumental*

4. I've got to move.
   Come, let me take you on a party ride,
   And I'll teach you, teach you, teach you,
   I'll teach you the electric slide.

Fight for Your Right
(To Party)

Registration 4
Rhythm: Rock

Words and Music by Rick Rubin,
Adam Horovitz and Adam Yauch

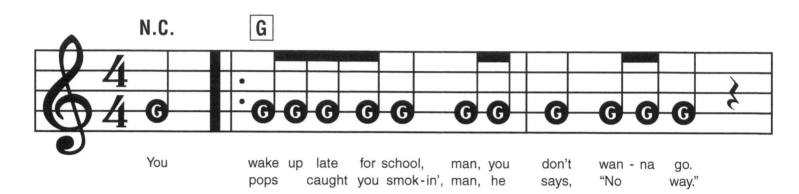

You wake up late for school, man, you don't wan-na go.
pops caught you smok-in', man, he says, "No way."

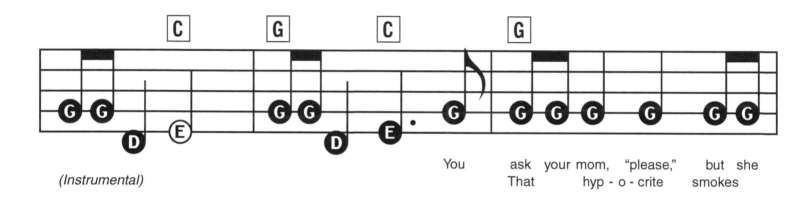

(Instrumental)

You ask your mom, "please," but she
That hyp-o-crite smokes

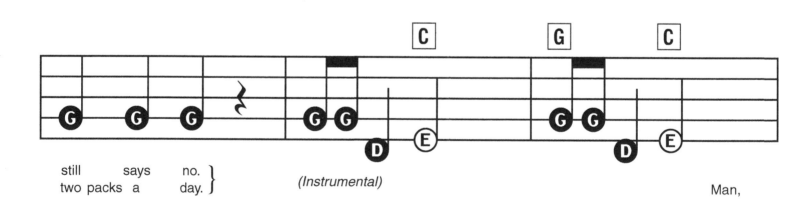

still says no. }
two packs a day. }

(Instrumental)

Man,

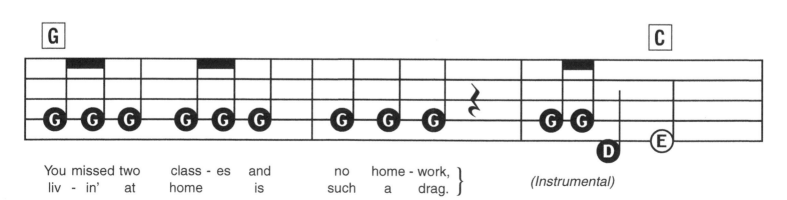

You missed two class-es and no home-work, }
liv-in' at home is such a drag. }

(Instrumental)

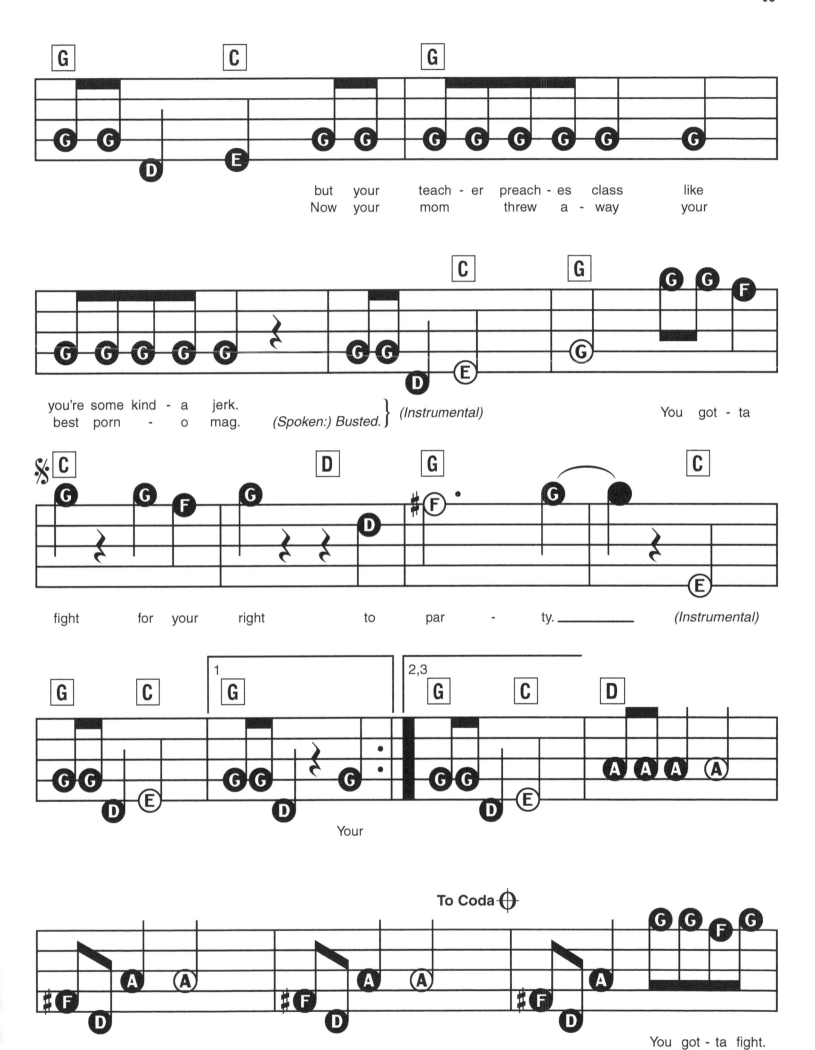

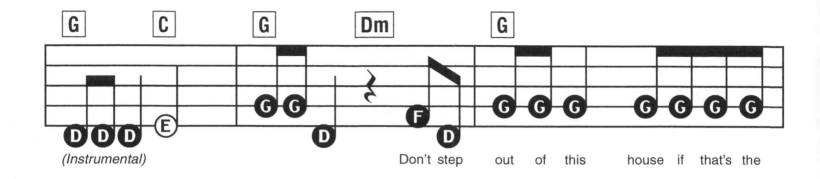

(Instrumental)

Don't step out of this house if that's the

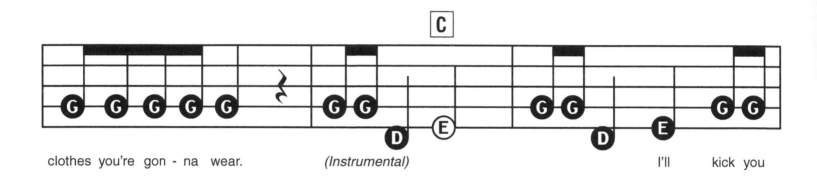

clothes you're gon - na wear.　(Instrumental)　I'll kick you

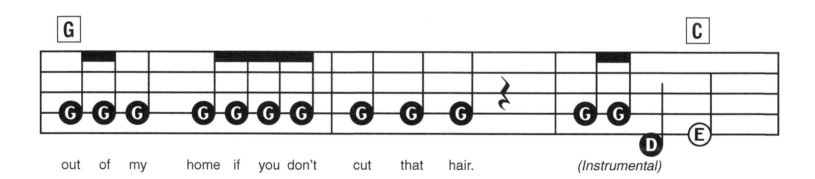

out of my home if you don't cut that hair.　(Instrumental)

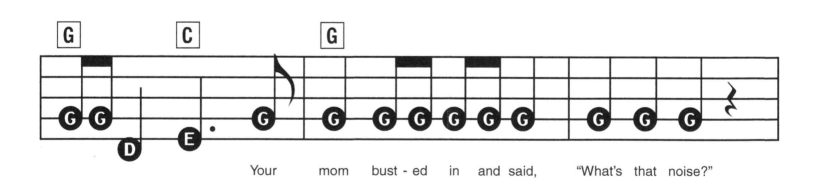

Your mom bust - ed in and said, "What's that noise?"

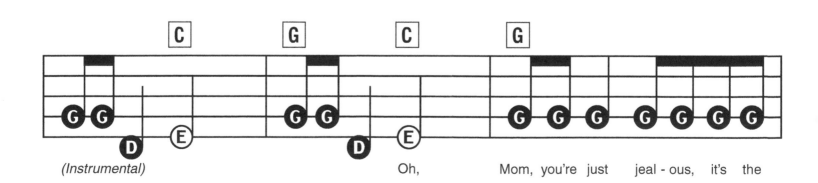

(Instrumental)　Oh,　Mom, you're just jeal - ous, it's the

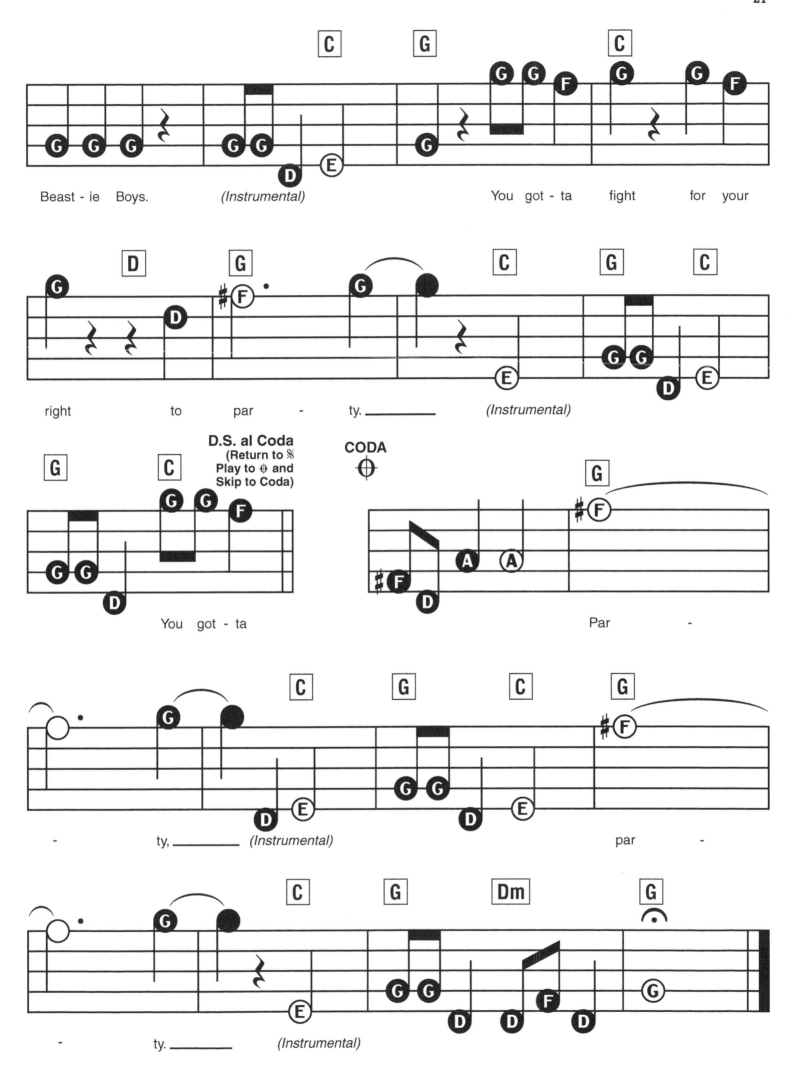

Get Down Tonight

Registration 4
Rhythm: 8 Beat or Rock

Words and Music by Harry Wayne Casey
and Richard Finch

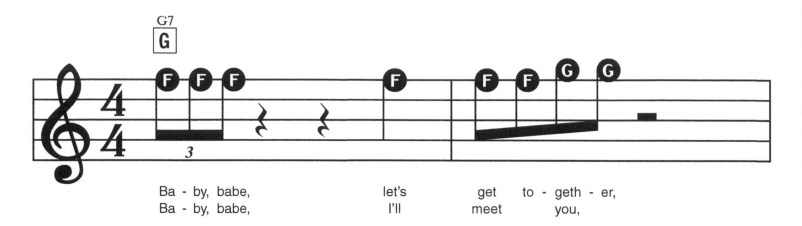

Ba - by, babe,   let's   get   to - geth - er,
Ba - by, babe,   I'll   get   meet   you,

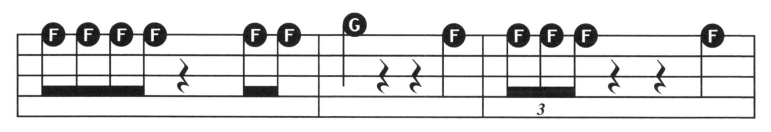

hon - ey, hon - ey,   me and   you,   and   do the things,   oh,
same   place,   same time _____   where   we   can,   oh,

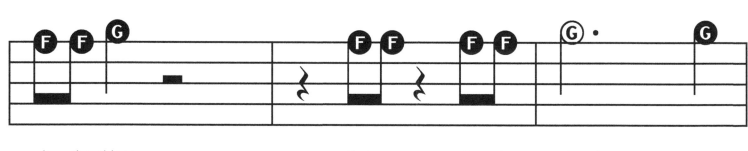

do   the things   that we   like to   do. }   Oh,
get   to - geth - er and   ease   up   our   mind.

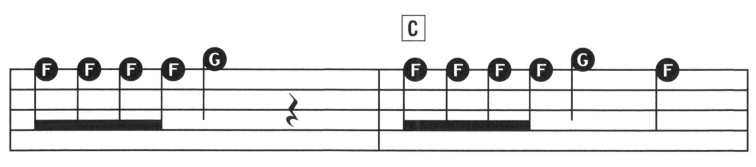

do   a   lit - tle dance,   make   a   lit - tle love,   get

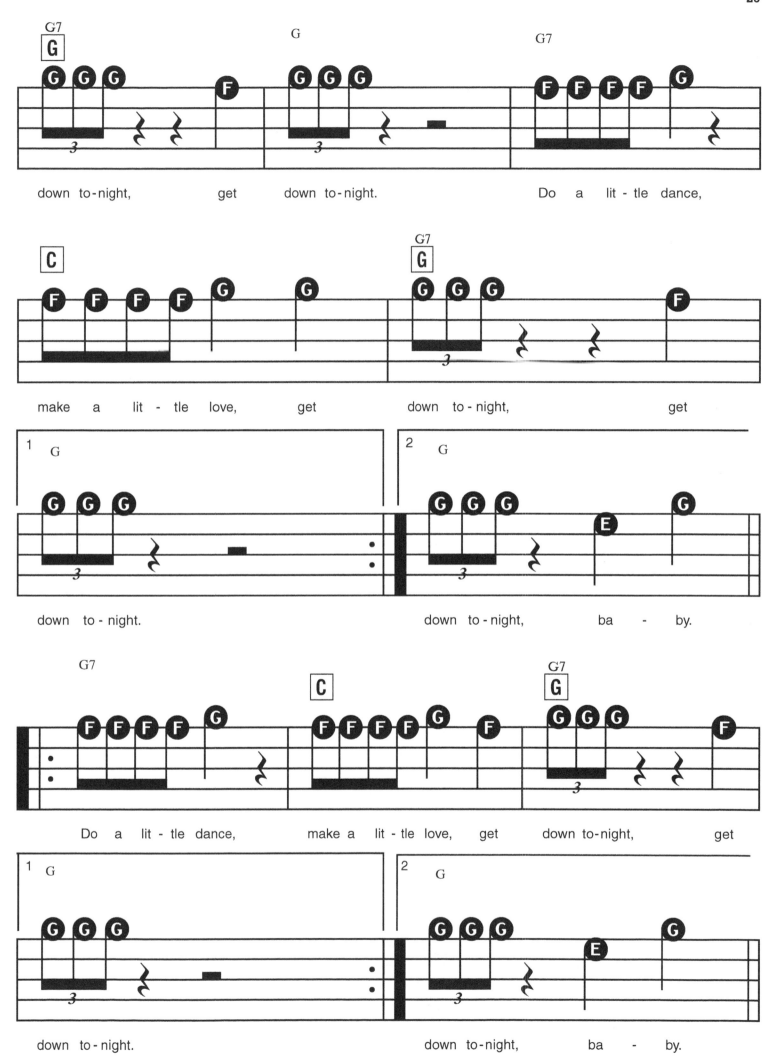

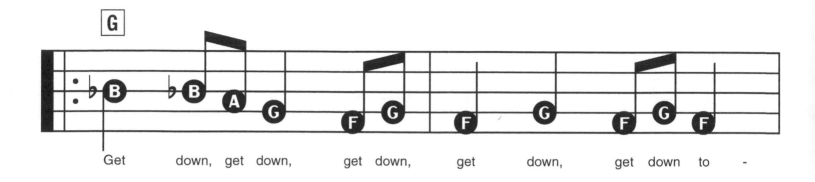

Get down, get down, get down, get down, get down to -

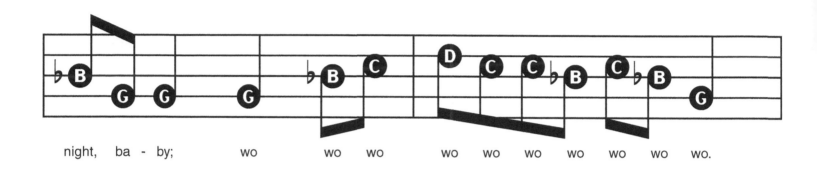

night, ba - by; wo wo wo wo wo wo wo wo wo wo.

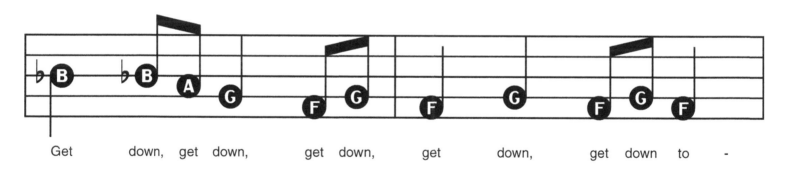

Get down, get down, get down, get down, get down to -

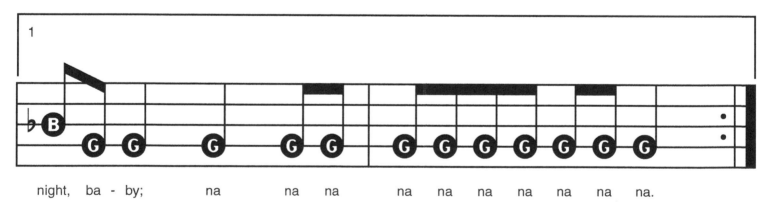

night, ba - by; na na na na na na na na na na.

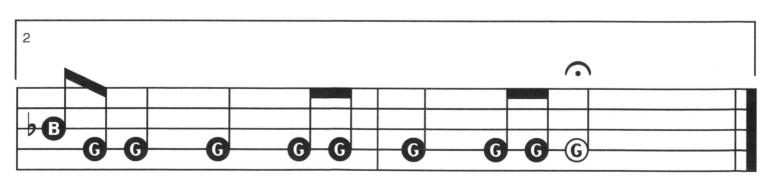

night, ba - by, this ver - y min - ute child, oh.

Girls Just Want to Have Fun

Registration 7
Rhythm: Rock

Words and Music by
Robert Hazard

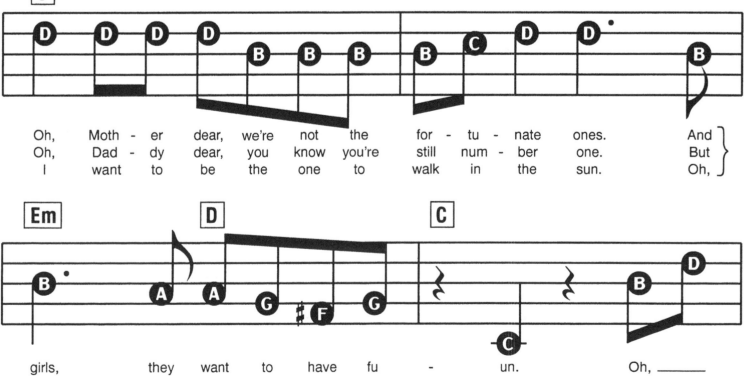

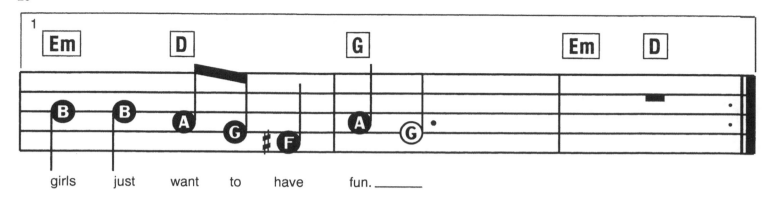

girls just want to have fun. _____

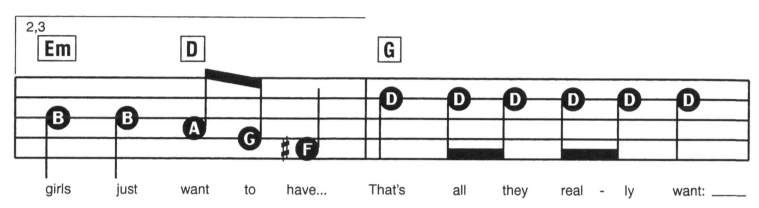

girls just want to have... That's all they real - ly want: _____

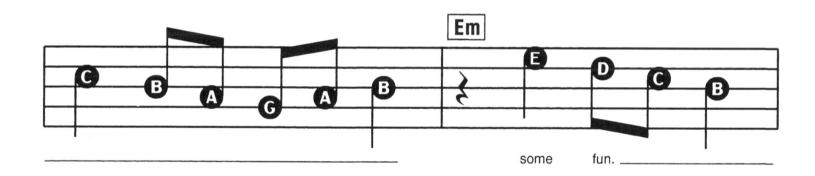

some fun. _____

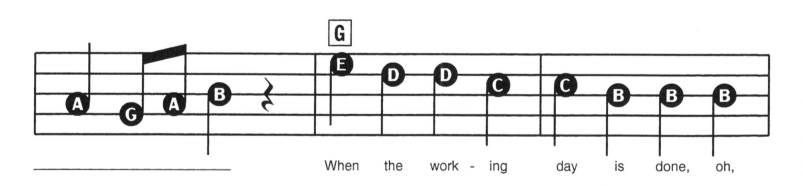

_____ When the work - ing day is done, oh,

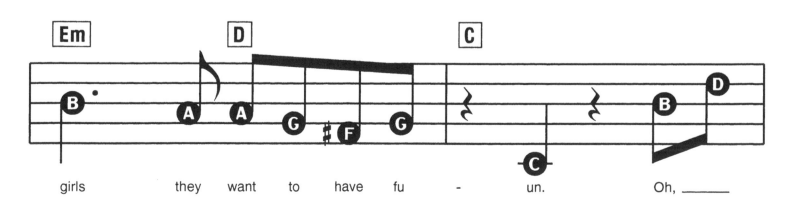

girls they want to have fu - un. Oh, _____

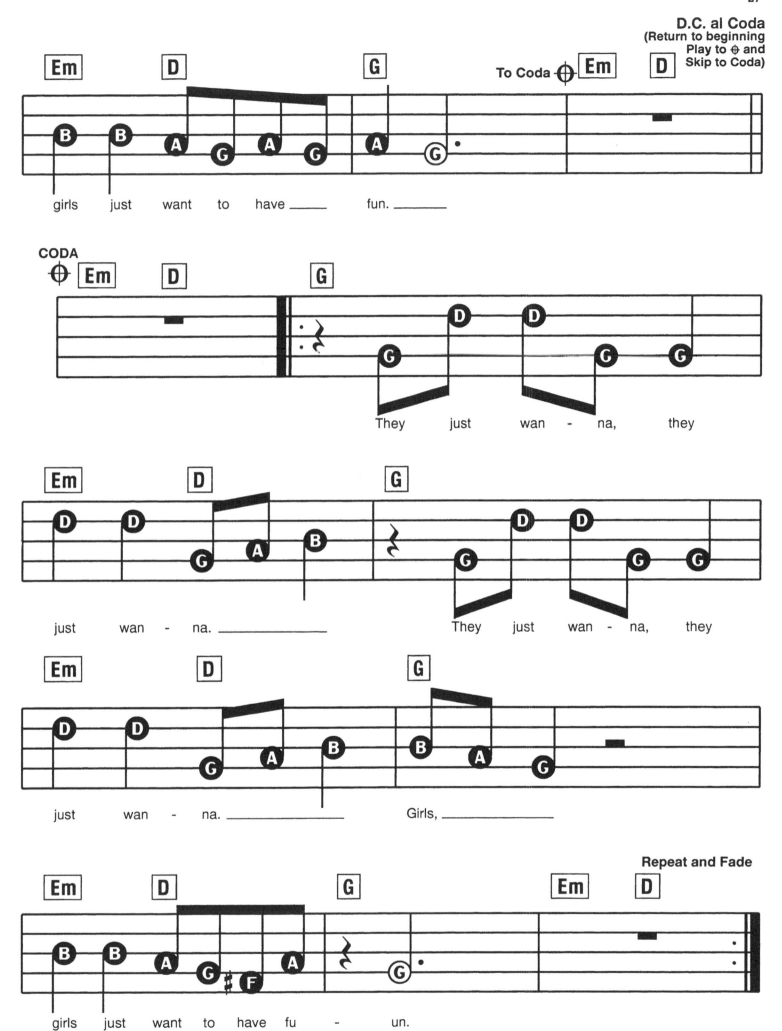

Hands Up
(Give Me Your Heart)

Registration 4
Rhythm: 8 Beat or Rock

Words and Music by Jean Kluger
and Daniel Vangarde
English Adaptation by Nellie Byl

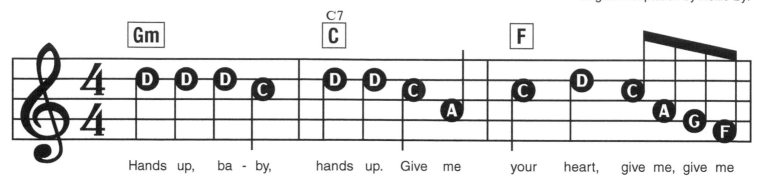

Hands up, ba - by, hands up. Give me your heart, give me, give me

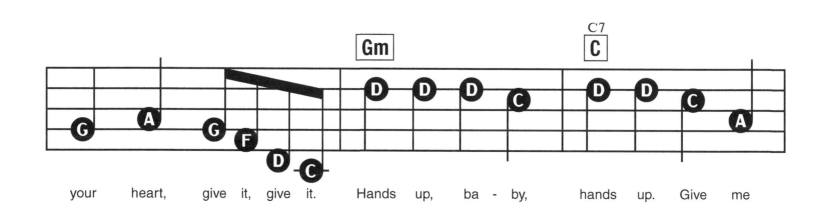

your heart, give it, give it. Hands up, ba - by, hands up. Give me

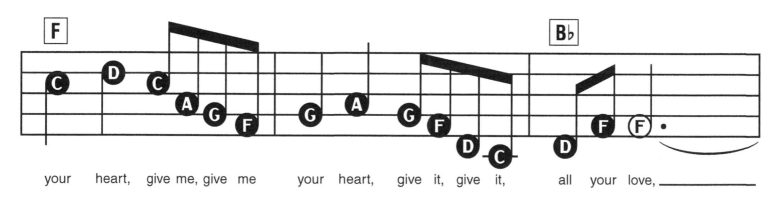

your heart, give me, give me your heart, give it, give it, all your love, _____

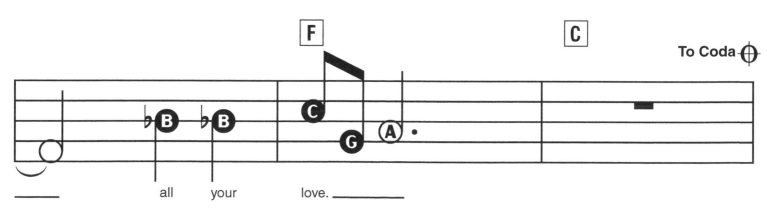

_____ all your love. _____

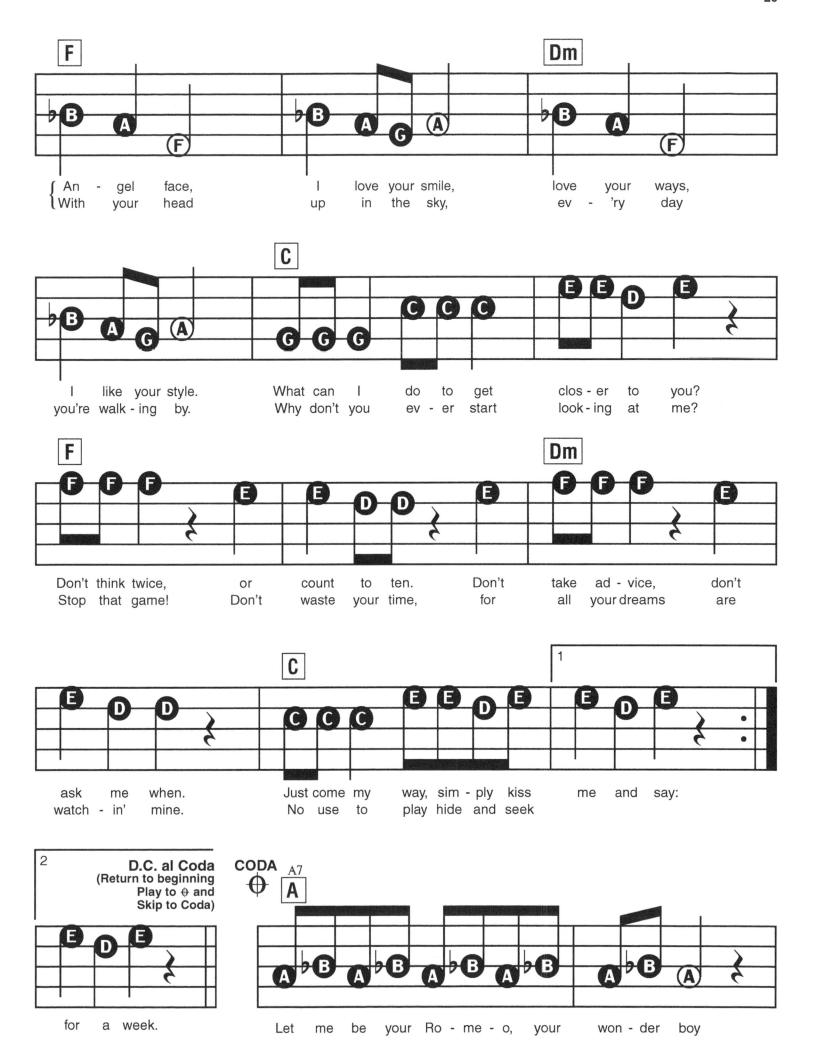

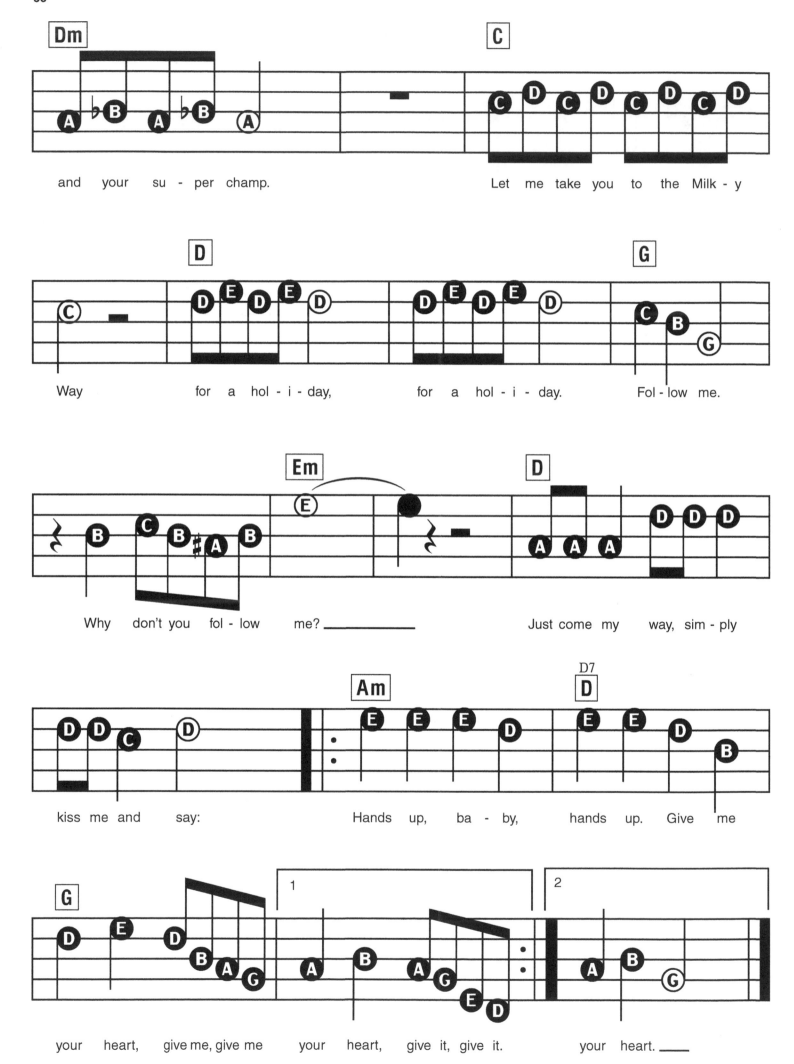

I Got You
(I Feel Good)

Registration 4
Rhythm: Rock or 8 Beat

Words and Music by
James Brown

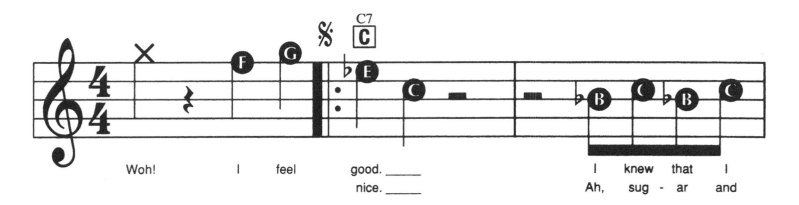

Woh!   I feel good. _____   I knew that I
nice. _____   Ah, sug - ar and

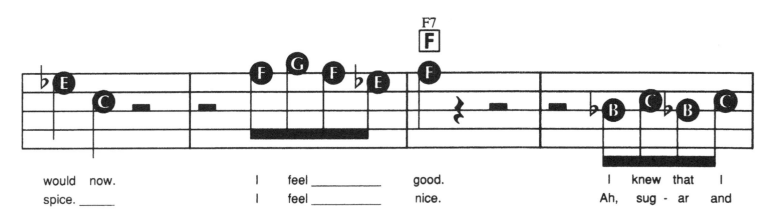

would now.   I feel _____ good.   I knew that I
spice. _____   I feel _____ nice.   Ah, sug - ar and

would now.   So good,   so good,   I got _____ you.
spice. _____   So nice,   so nice,   I got _____ you.

To Coda ⊕

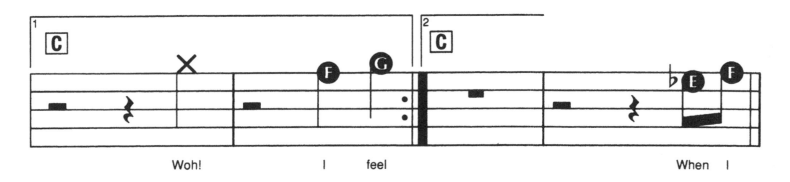

Woh!   I feel   When I

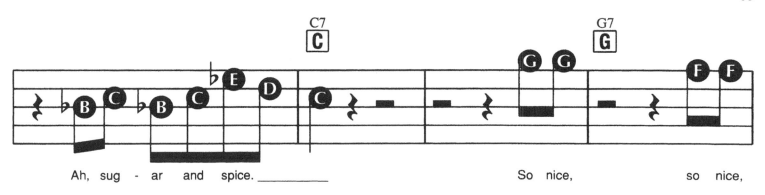

Ah, sug - ar and spice. _____ So nice, so nice,

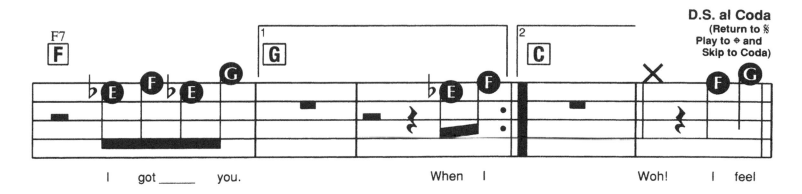

I got _____ you. When I Woh! I feel

D.S. al Coda
(Return to %
Play to ⊕ and
Skip to Coda)

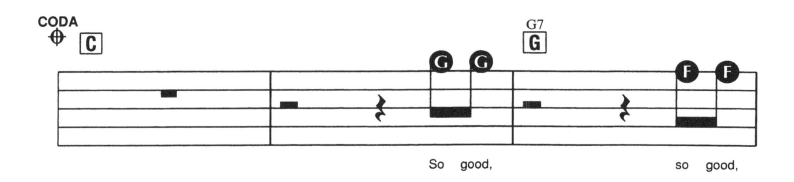

CODA

So good, so good,

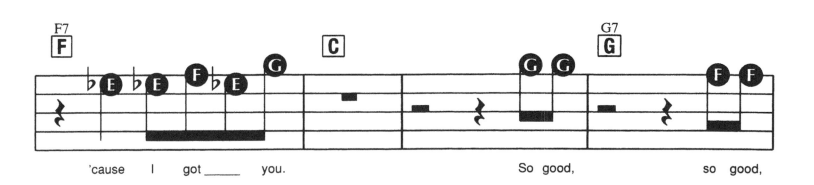

'cause I got _____ you. So good, so good,

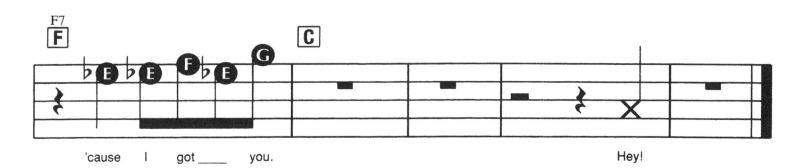

'cause I got _____ you. Hey!

The Hokey Pokey

Registration 5
Rhythm: Fox Trot or Swing

Words and Music by Charles P. Macak,
Tafft Baker and Larry LaPrise

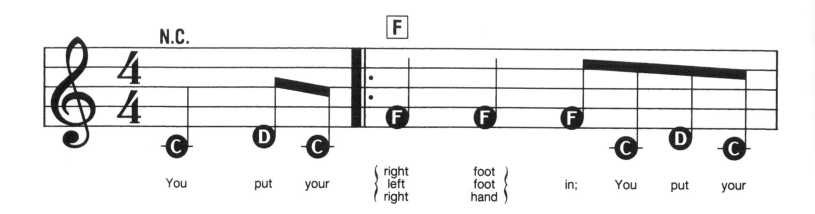

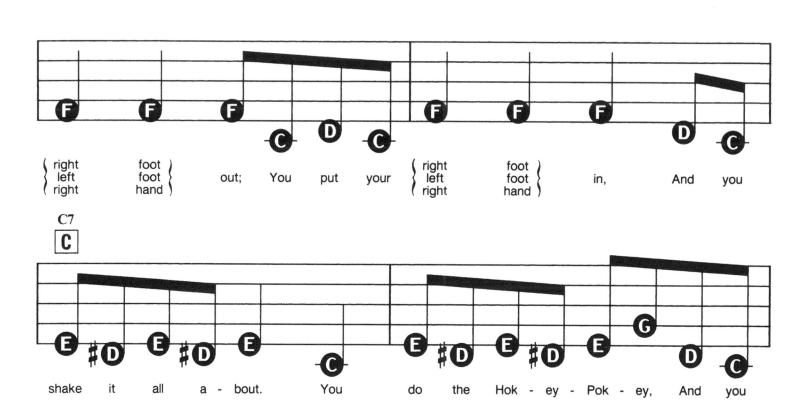

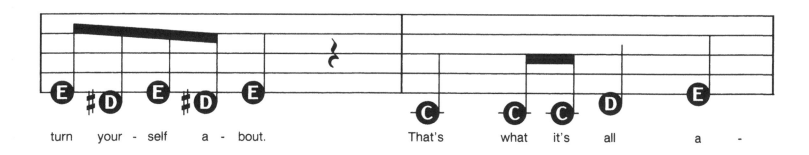

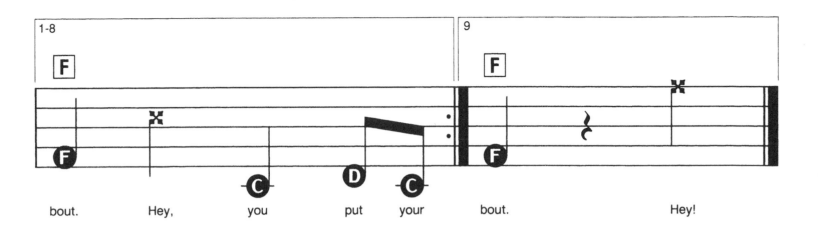

bout.   Hey,   you   put   your   bout.   Hey!

Additional Lyrics

4. Hey, you put your left hand in;
   You put your left hand out;
   You put your left hand in,
   And you shake it all about.
   You do the Hokey-Pokey,
   And you turn yourself about.
   That's what it's all about.

5. Hey, you put your right shoulder in;
   You put your right shoulder out;
   Etc.

6. Hey, you put your left shoulder in;
   You put your left shoulder out;
   Etc.

7. Hey, you put your right hip in;
   You put your right hip out;
   Etc.

8. Hey, you put your left hip in;
   You put your left hip out;
   Etc.

9. Hey, you put your whole self in;
   You put your whole self out;
   Etc.

Hot Hot Hot

Registration 5
Rhythm: Dance or Rock

Words and Music by
Alphonsus Cassell

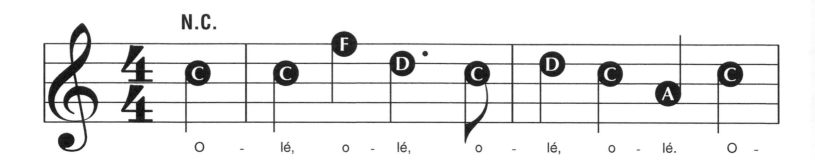

O - lé, o - lé, o - lé, o - lé. O -

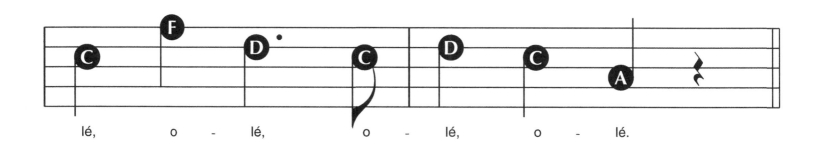

lé, o - lé, o - lé, o - lé.

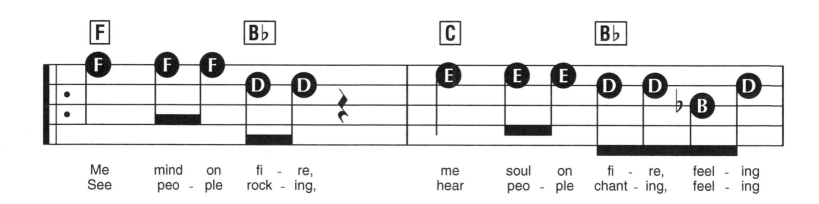

Me mind on fi - re, me soul on fi - re, feel - ing
See peo - ple rock - ing, hear peo - ple chant - ing, feel - ing

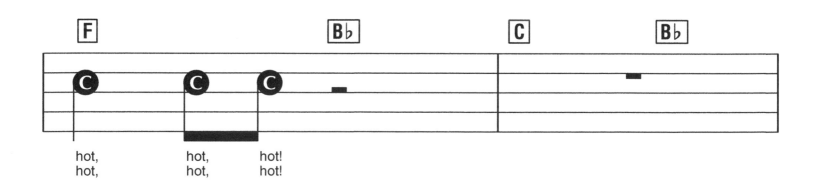

hot, hot, hot!
hot, hot, hot!

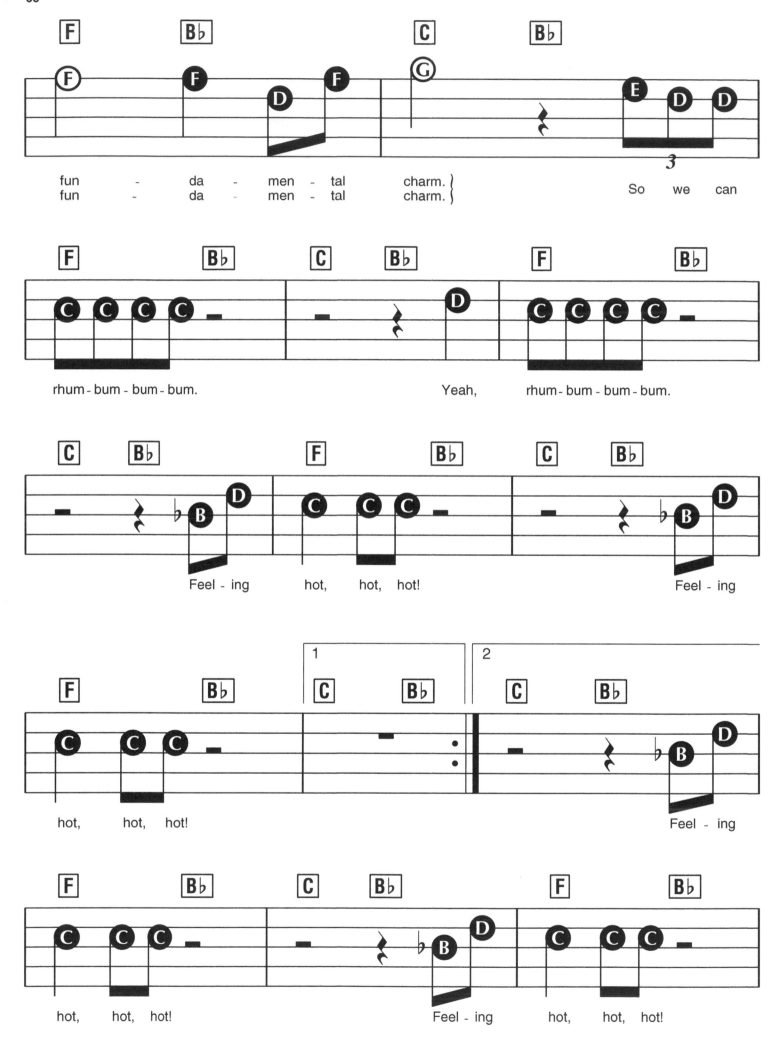

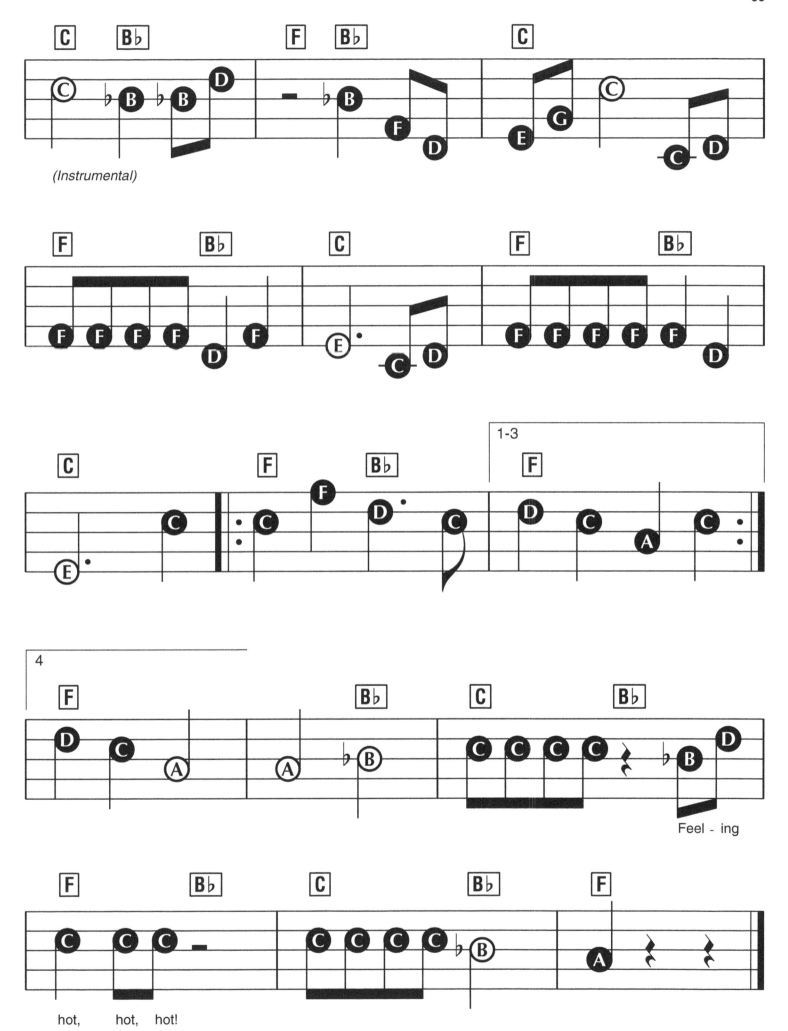

(Instrumental)

Feel - ing

hot, hot, hot!

I Love Rock 'n Roll

Registration 3
Rhythm: Rock

Words and Music by Alan Merrill
and Jake Hooker

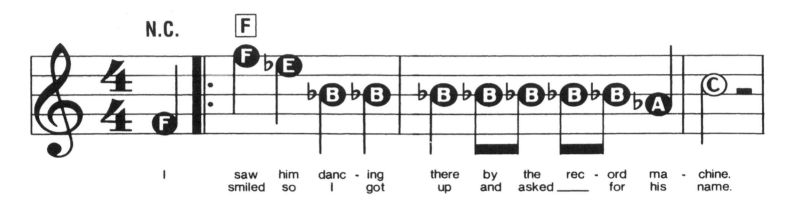

I saw him danc - ing there by the rec - ord ma - chine.
smiled so I got up and asked _____ for his name.

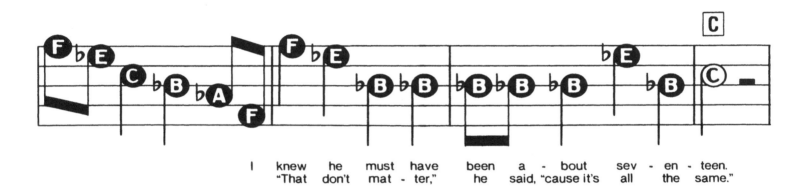

I knew he must have been a - bout sev - en - teen.
"That don't mat - ter," he said, "cause it's all the same."

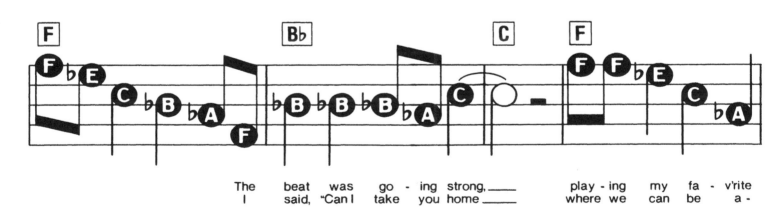

The beat was go - ing strong, _____ play - ing my fa - v'rite
I said, "Can I take you home _____ where we can be a -

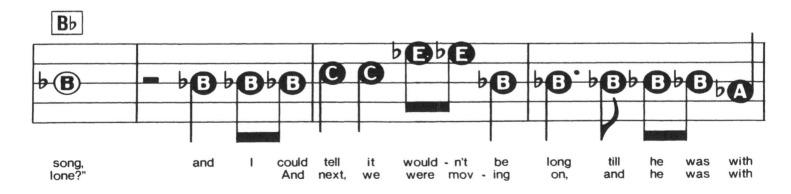

song, and I could tell it would - n't be long till he was with
lone?" And next, we were mov - ing on, and he was with

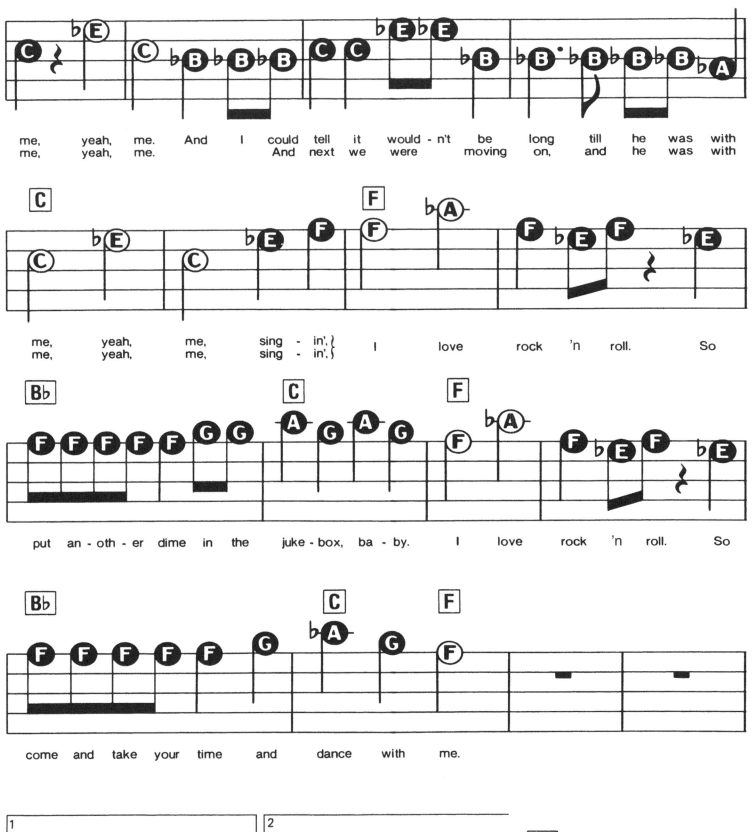

me,   yeah,   me.   And   I   could   tell   it   would - n't   be   long,   till   he   was   with
me,   yeah,   me.   And   next   we   were   moving   on,   and   he   was   with

me,   yeah,   me,   sing - in', }   I   love   rock   'n   roll.   So

put   an - oth - er   dime   in   the   juke - box,   ba - by.   I   love   rock   'n   roll.   So

come   and   take   your   time   and   dance   with   me.

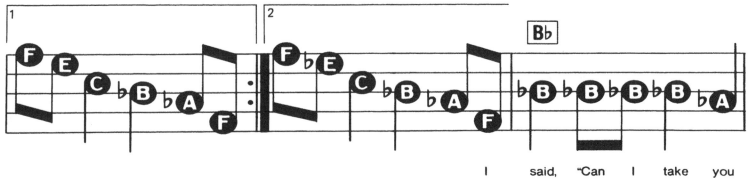

I   said,   "Can   I   take   you

41

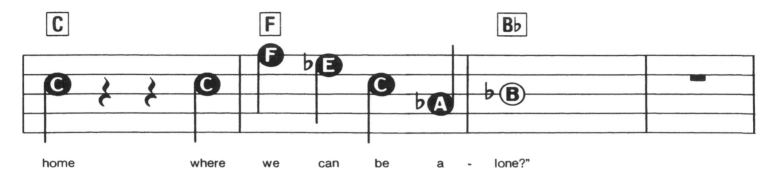

home where we can be a - lone?"

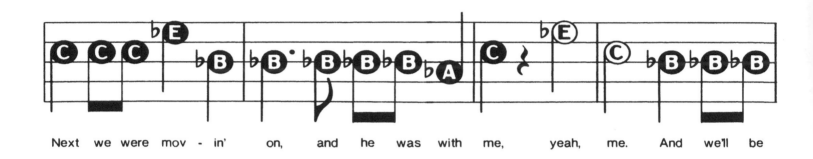

Next we were mov - in' on, and he was with me, yeah, me. And we'll be

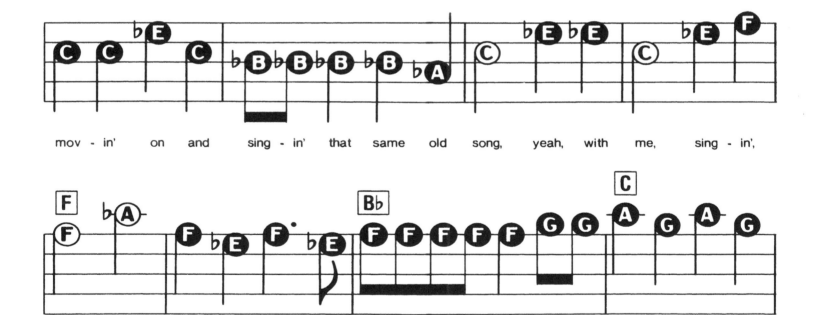

mov - in' on and sing - in' that same old song, yeah, with me, sing - in',

I love rock 'n roll. So put an - oth - er dime in the juke - box, ba - by.

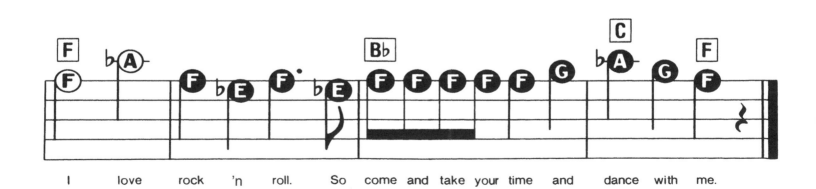

I love rock 'n roll. So come and take your time and dance with me.

I'm So Excited

Registration 1
Rhythm: Rock or Disco

Words and Music by Trevor Lawrence, June Pointer,
Ruth Pointer and Anita Pointer

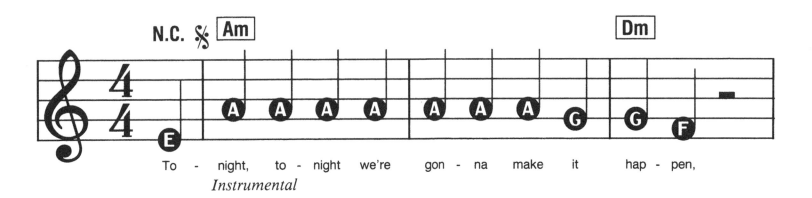

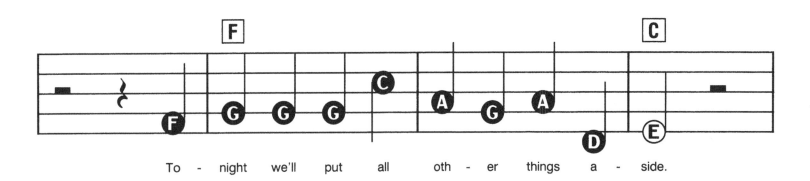

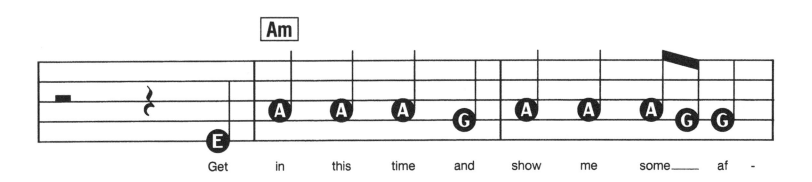

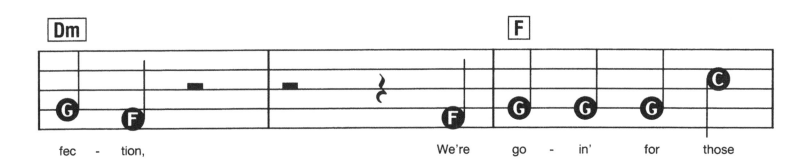

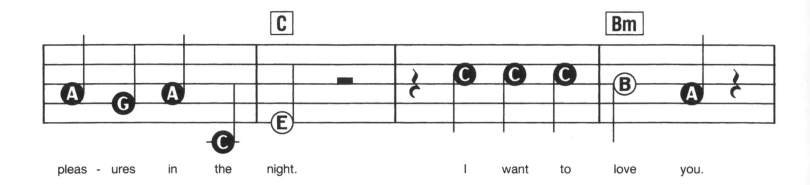

pleas - ures   in   the   night.   I   want   to   love   you.

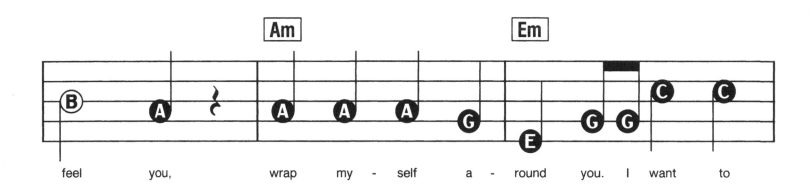

feel   you,   wrap   my - self   a - round   you.   I   want   to

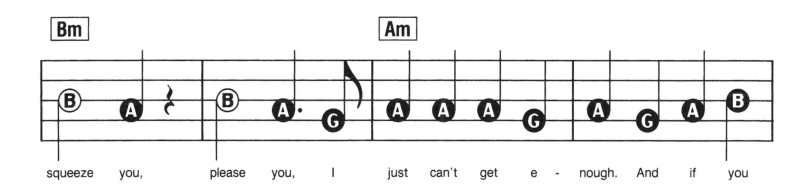

squeeze   you,   please   you,   I   just   can't   get   e - nough.   And   if   you

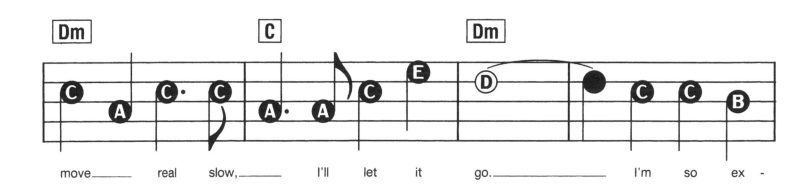

move_____ real   slow,_____   I'll   let   it   go._____   I'm   so   ex -

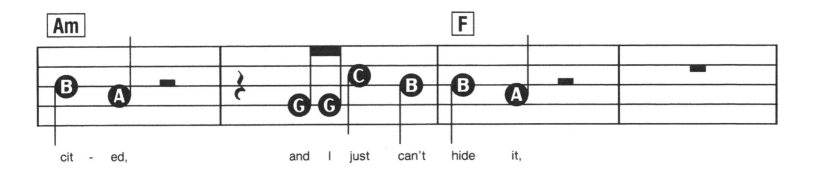

Am   F

cit - ed,   and I just can't hide it,

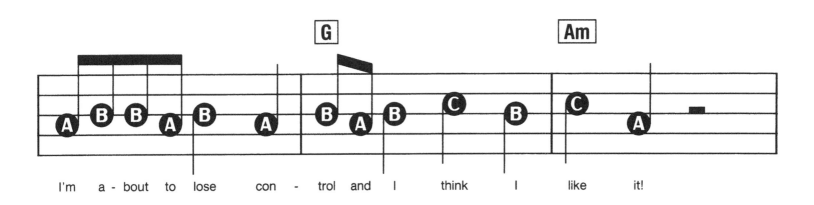

G   Am

I'm a - bout to lose con - trol and I think I like it!

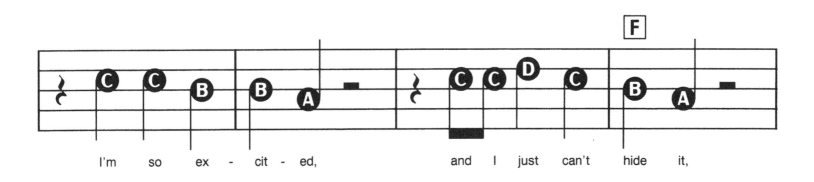

F

I'm so ex - cit - ed,   and I just can't hide it,

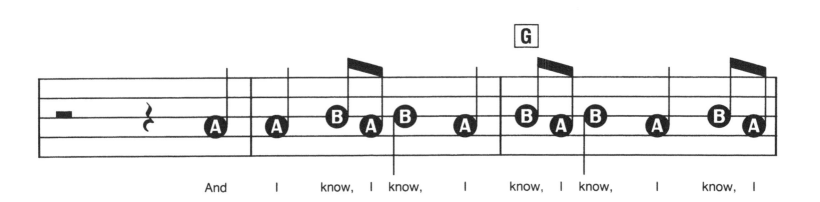

G

And I know, I know, I know, I know, I know, I

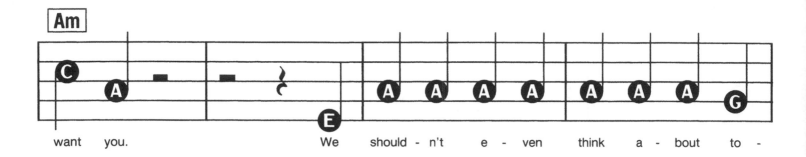

want you.   We   should - n't   e - ven   think   a - bout   to -

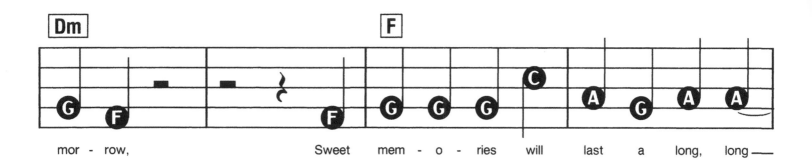

mor - row,   Sweet   mem - o - ries   will   last   a   long,   long

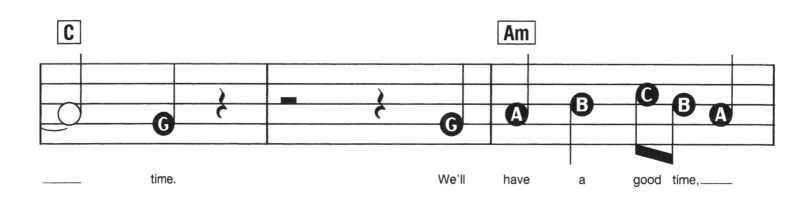

_____   time.   We'll   have   a   good   time,____

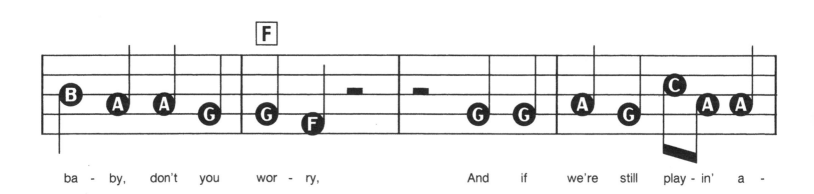

ba - by,   don't   you   wor - ry,   And   if   we're   still   play - in' a -

47

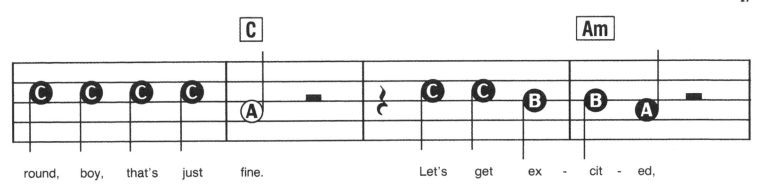

round, boy, that's just fine.   Let's get ex - cit - ed,

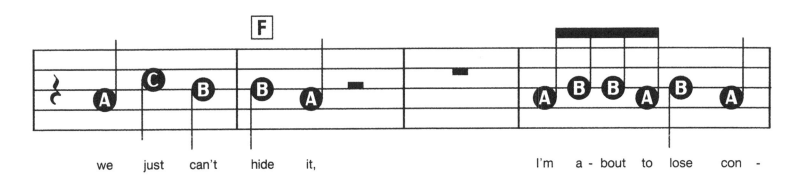

we just can't hide it,   I'm a - bout to lose con -

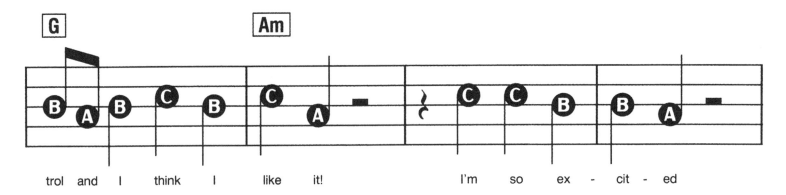

trol and I think I like it!   I'm so ex - cit - ed

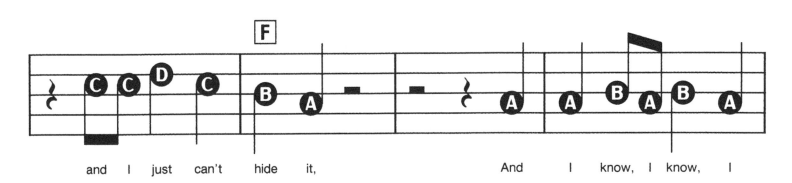

and I just can't hide it,   And I know, I know, I

D.S. and Fade
(Return to %
and fade)

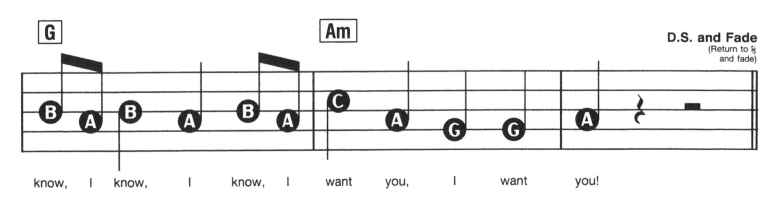

know, I know, I know, I want you, I want you!

I Will Survive

Registration 5
Rhythm: Rock or Disco

Words and Music by Dino Fekaris
and Frederick J. Perren

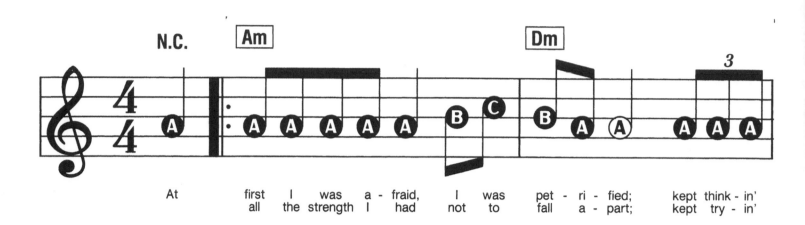

At first I was a-fraid, I was pet-ri-fied; kept think-in'
all the strength I had not to fall a-part; kept try-in'

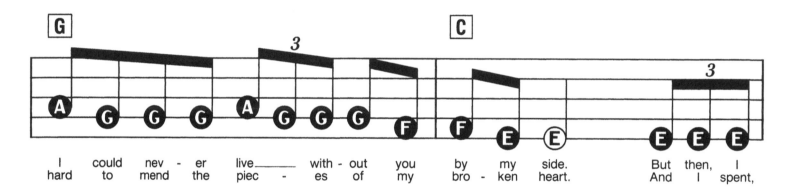

I could nev-er live_____ with-out you by my side. But then, I
hard to mend the piec-es of my bro-ken heart. And I spent,

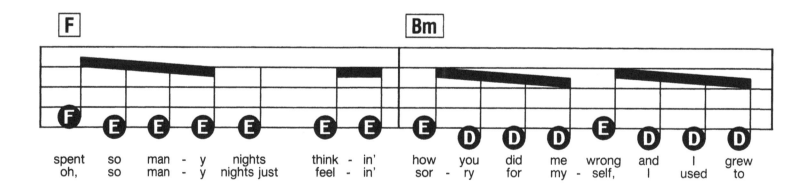

spent so man-y nights think-in' how you did me wrong and I grew
oh, so man-y nights just feel-in' sor-ry for my-self, I used to

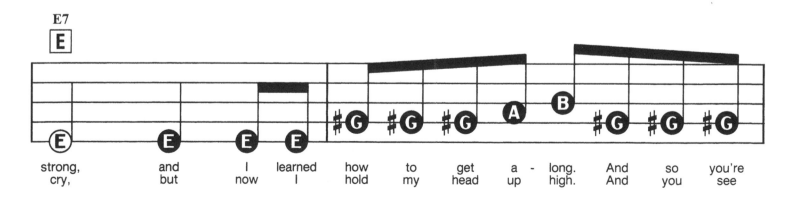

strong, and I learned how to get a-long. And so you're
cry, but now I hold my head up high. And you see

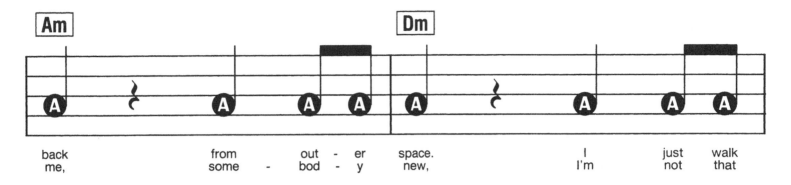

back from out - er space. I just walk
me, some - bod - y new, I'm not that

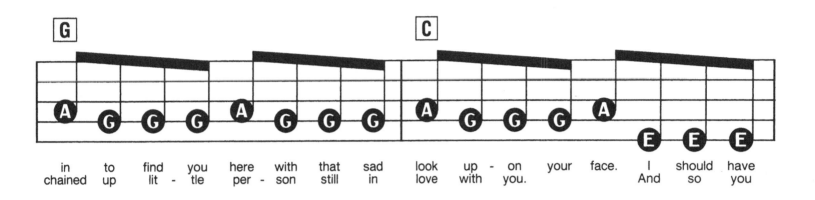

in to find you here with that sad look up - on your face. I should have
chained up lit - tle per - son still in love with you. And so you

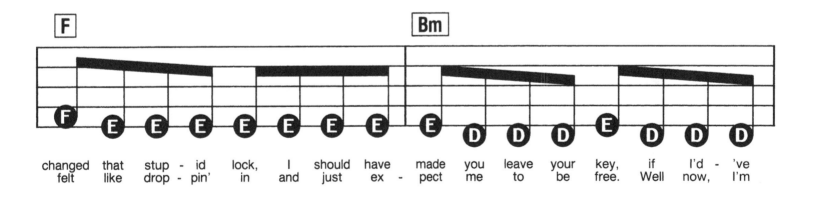

changed that stup - id lock, I should have made you leave your key, if I'd - 've
felt like drop - pin' in and just ex - pect me to be free. Well now, I'm

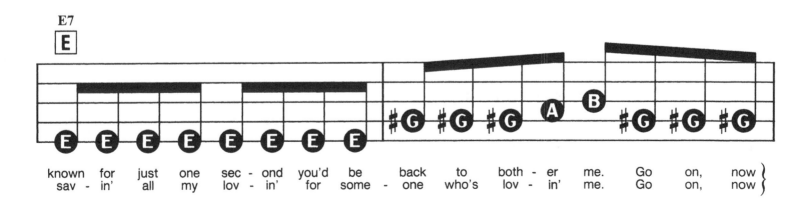

known for just one sec - ond you'd be back to both - er me. Go on, now
sav - in' all my lov - in' for some - one who's lov - in' me. Go on, now

50

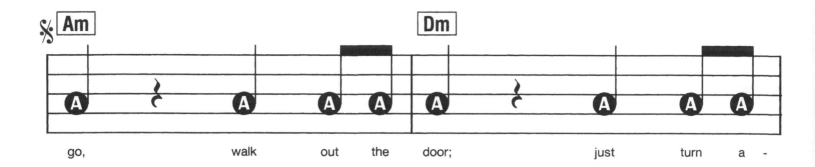

go, walk out the door; just turn a -

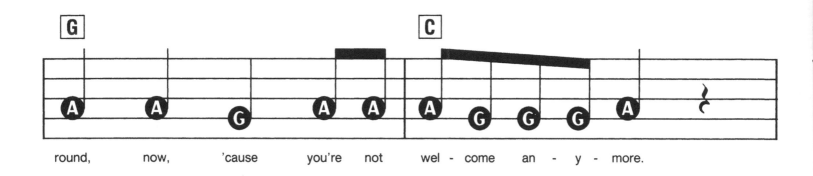

round, now, 'cause you're not wel - come an - y - more.

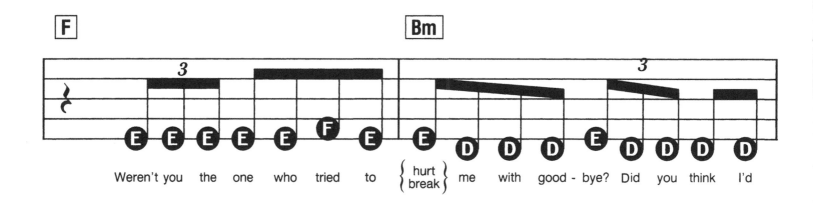

Weren't you the one who tried to { hurt / break } me with good - bye? Did you think I'd

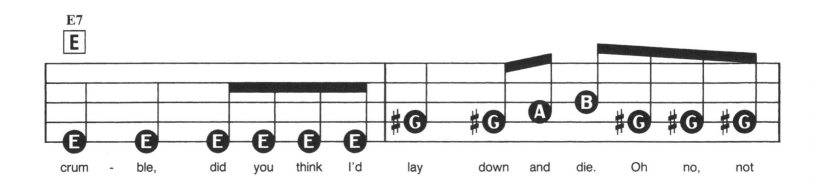

crum - ble, did you think I'd lay down and die. Oh no, not

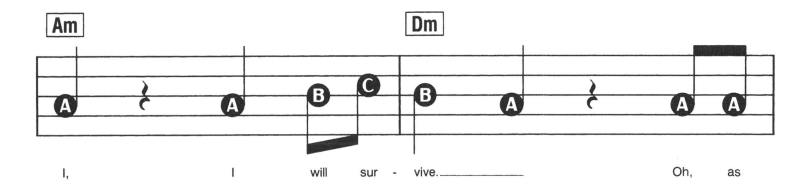

I,   I   will sur - vive._____   Oh,   as

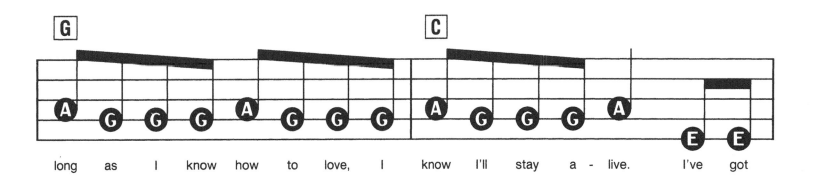

long   as   I   know   how   to   love,   I   know   I'll   stay   a - live.   I've   got

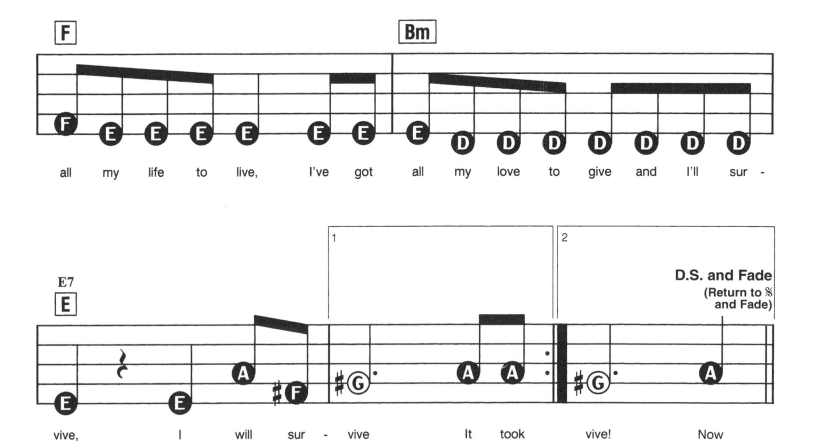

all   my   life   to   live,   I've   got   all   my   love   to   give   and   I'll   sur -

vive,   I   will   sur - vive   It   took   vive!   Now

I'm Too Sexy

Registration 2
Rhythm: Disco or Rock

Words and Music by Fred Fairbrass,
Richard Fairbrass and Robert Manzoli

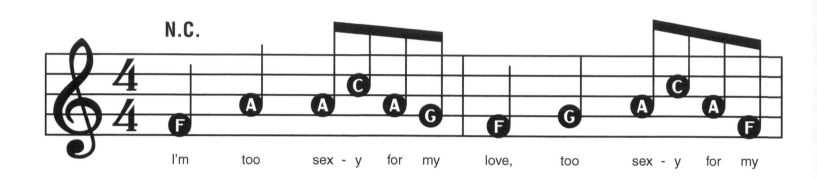

I'm too sex - y for my love, too sex - y for my

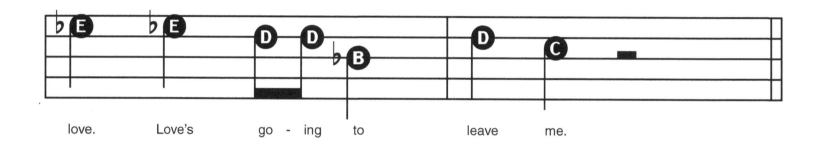

love. Love's go - ing to leave me.

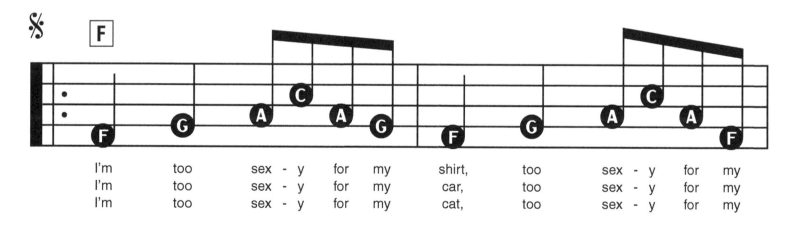

I'm too sex - y for my shirt, too sex - y for my
I'm too sex - y for my car, too sex - y for my
I'm too sex - y for my cat, too sex - y for my

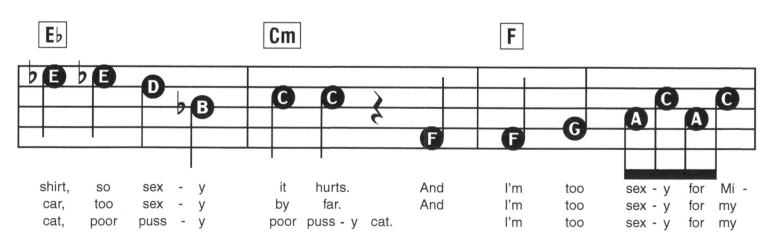

shirt, so sex - y it hurts. And I'm too sex - y for Mi -
car, too sex - y by far. And I'm too sex - y for my
cat, poor puss - y poor puss - y cat. I'm too sex - y for my

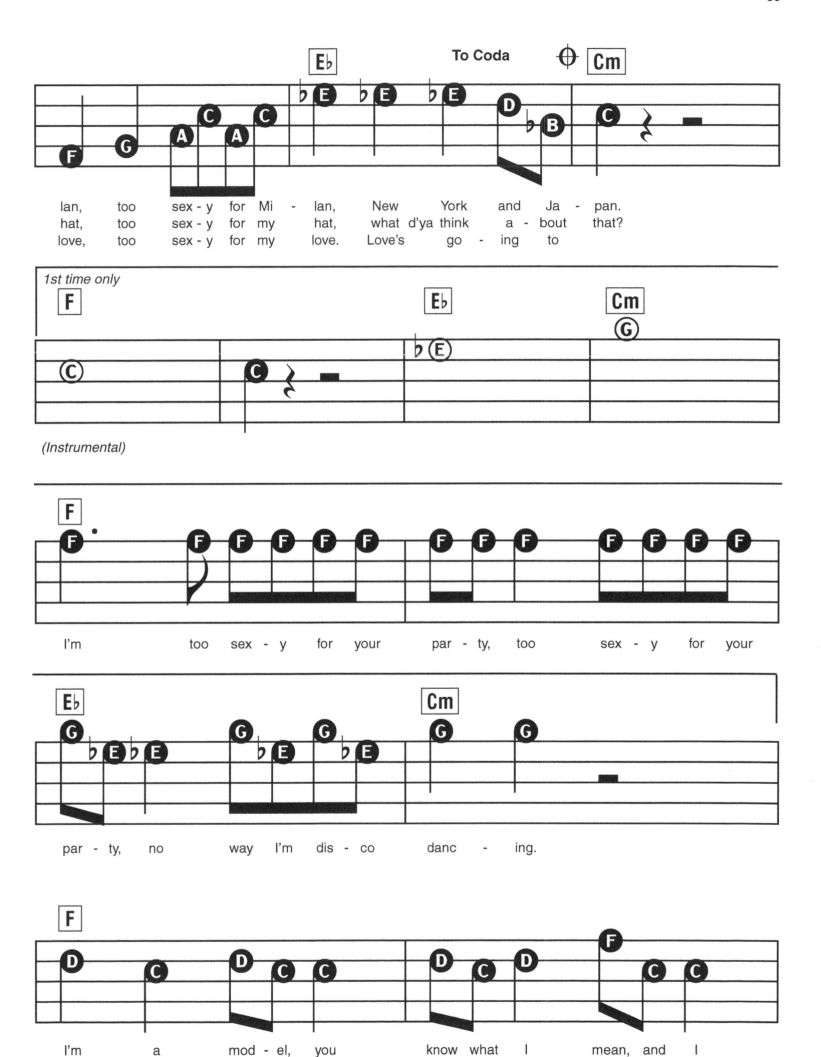

lan,   too   sex - y   for   Mi - lan,   New   York   and   Ja - pan.
hat,   too   sex - y   for   my   hat,   what d'ya think   a - bout   that?
love,   too   sex - y   for   my   love.   Love's   go - ing   to

1st time only

(Instrumental)

I'm   too   sex - y   for   your   par - ty, too   sex - y   for   your

par - ty,   no   way   I'm   dis - co   danc - ing.

I'm   a   mod - el,   you   know what   I   mean, and   I

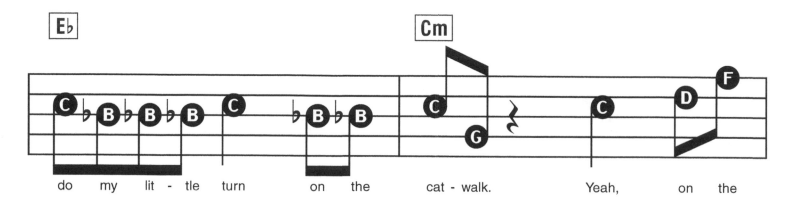

do my lit - tle turn on the cat - walk. Yeah, on the

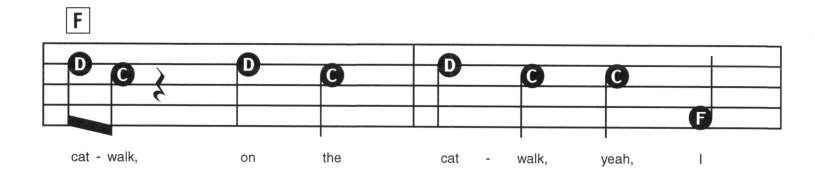

cat - walk, on the cat - walk, yeah, I

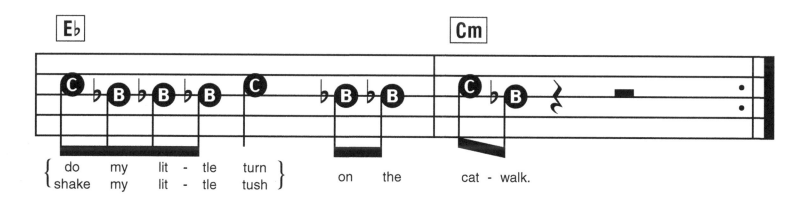

{ do my lit - tle turn }
{ shake my lit - tle tush }
on the cat - walk.

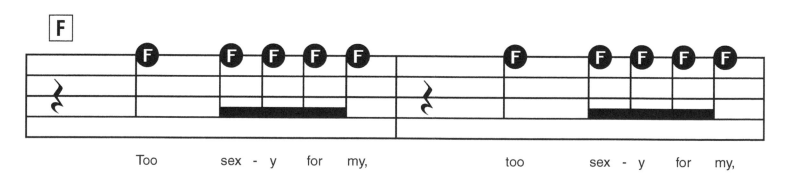

Too sex - y for my, too sex - y for my,

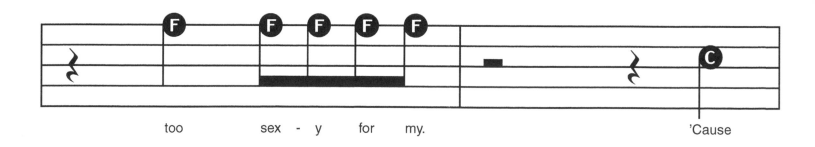

too sex - y for my. 'Cause

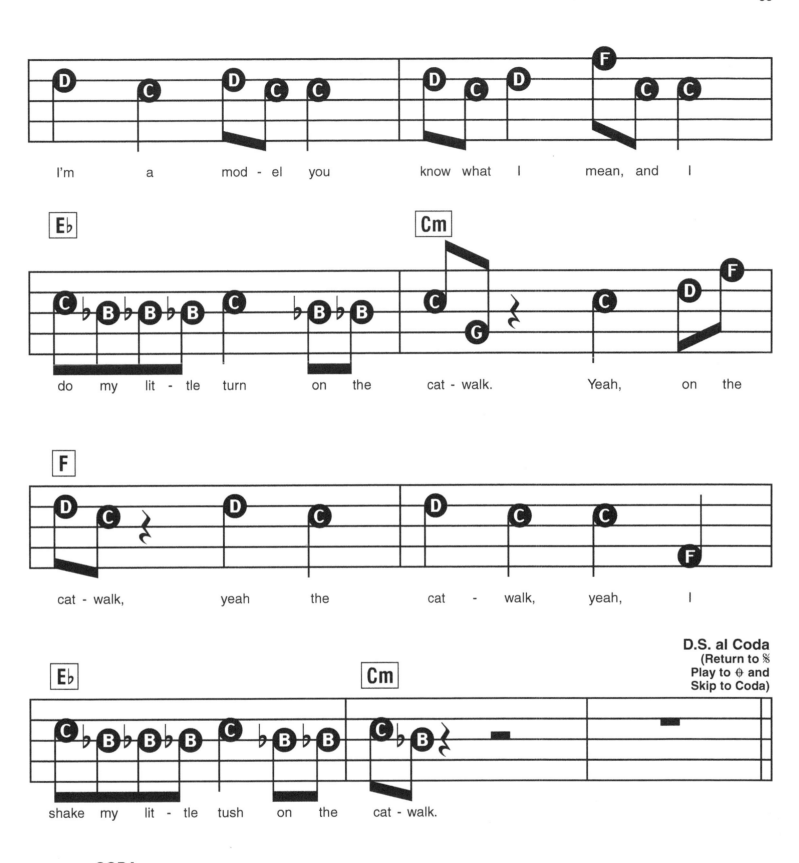

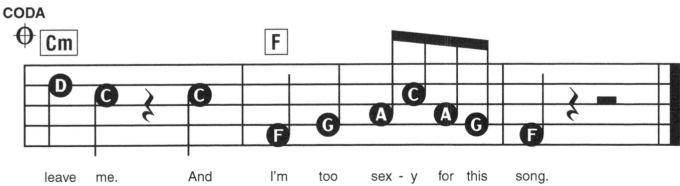

Joy to the World

Registration 2
Rhythm: Rock

Words and Music by
Hoyt Axton

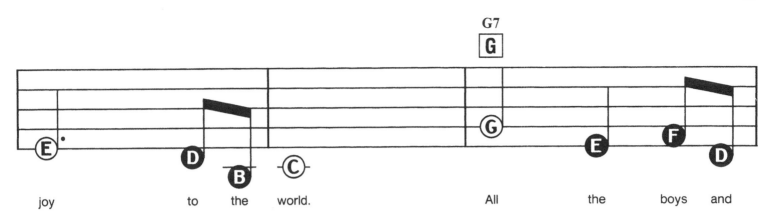

joy   to   the   world.   All   the   boys   and

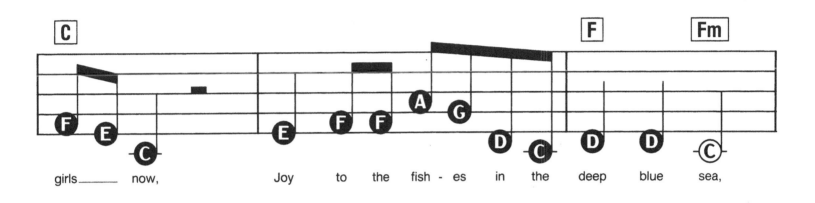

girls____ now,   Joy   to   the fish - es   in   the   deep blue sea,

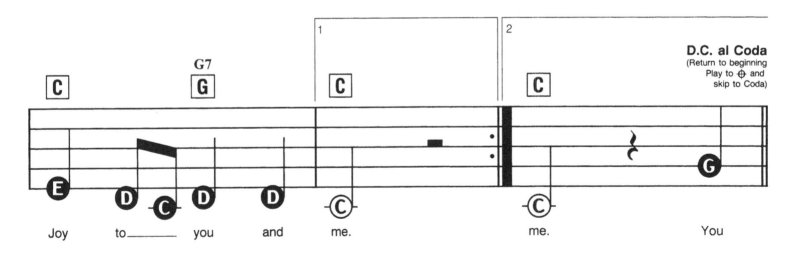

Joy   to____ you   and   me.   me.   You

D.C. al Coda
(Return to beginning
Play to ⊕ and
skip to Coda)

CODA

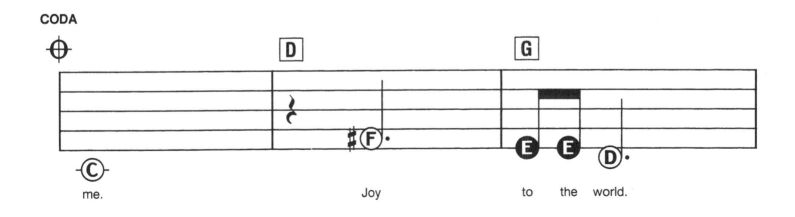

me.   Joy   to   the   world.

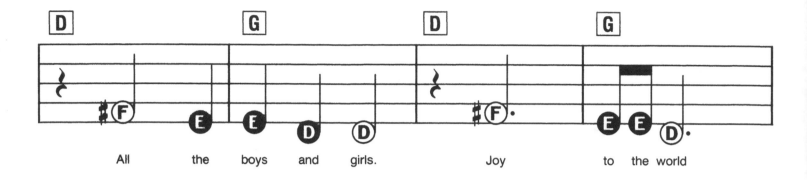

All the boys and girls. Joy to the world

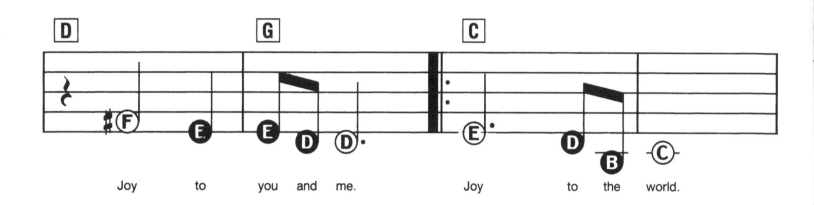

Joy to you and me. Joy to the world.

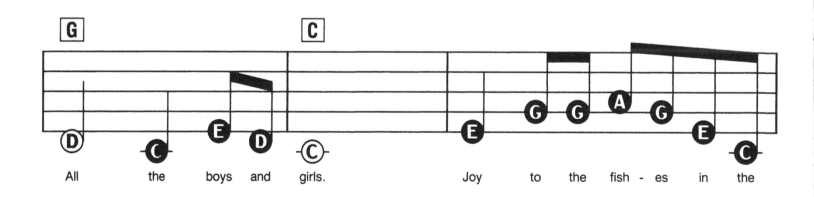

All the boys and girls. Joy to the fish - es in the

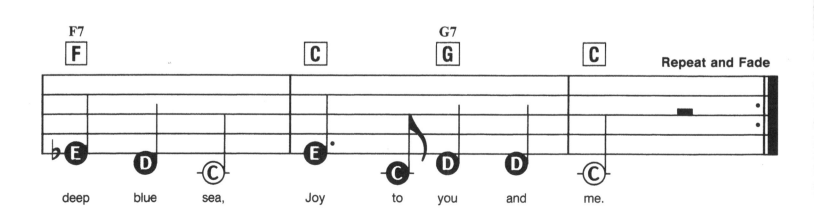

deep blue sea, Joy to you and me.

Jump, Jive an' Wail

Registration 4
Rhythm: Swing

Words and Music by
Louis Prima

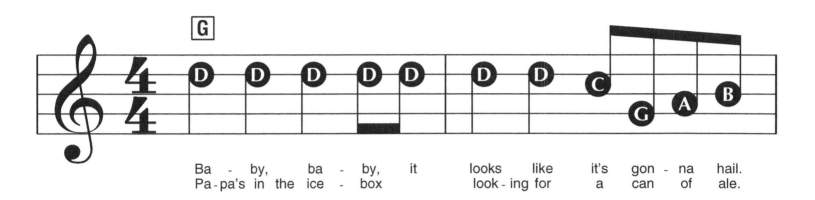

Ba - by, ba - by, it looks like it's gon - na hail.
Pa - pa's in the ice - box look - ing for a can of ale.

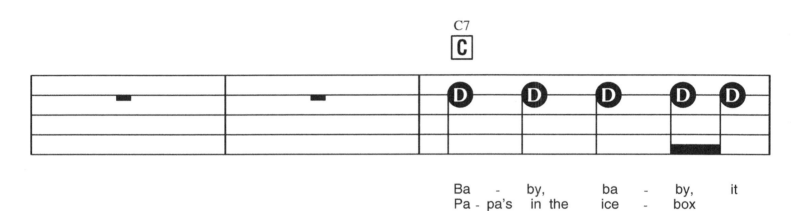

Ba - by, ba - by, it
Pa - pa's in the ice - box

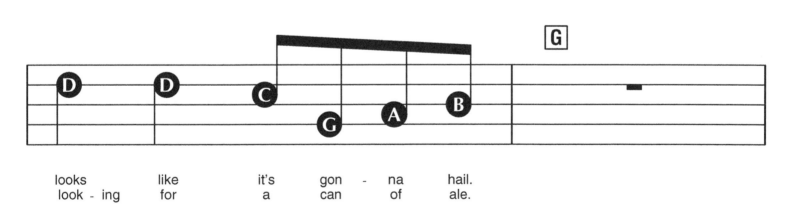

looks like it's gon - na hail.
look - ing for a can of ale.

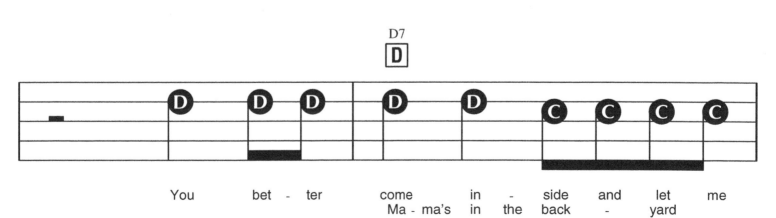

You bet - ter come in - side and let me
Ma - ma's in the back - yard

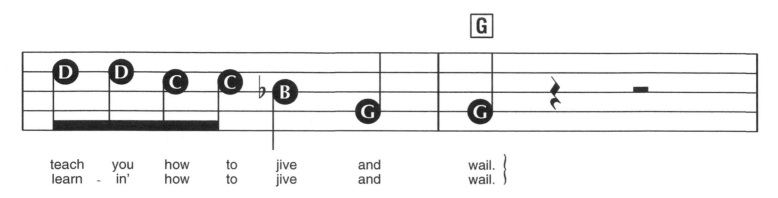

teach you how to jive and wail.
learn - in' how to jive and wail.

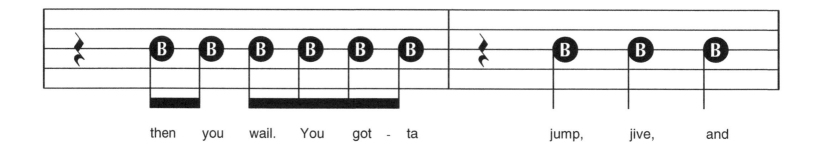

Oh, you got - ta jump, jive, and

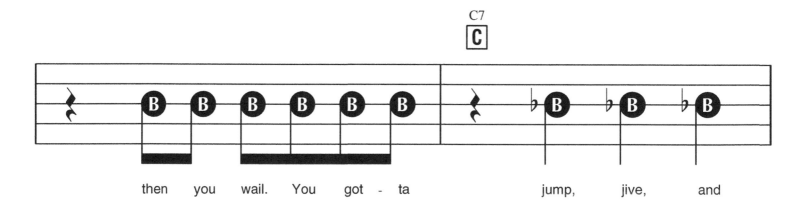

then you wail. You got - ta jump, jive, and

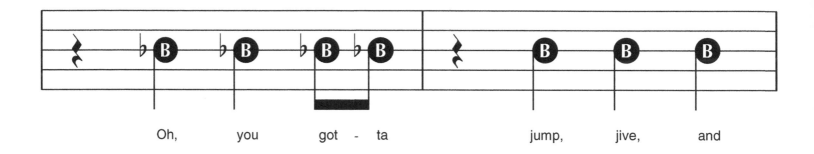

then you wail. You got - ta jump, jive, and

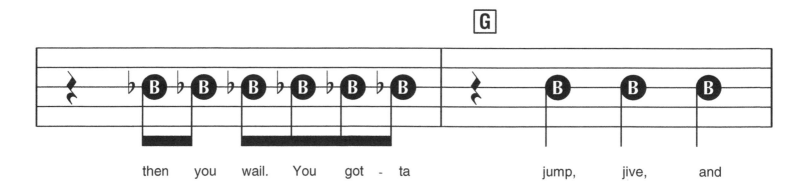

then you wail. You got - ta jump, jive, and

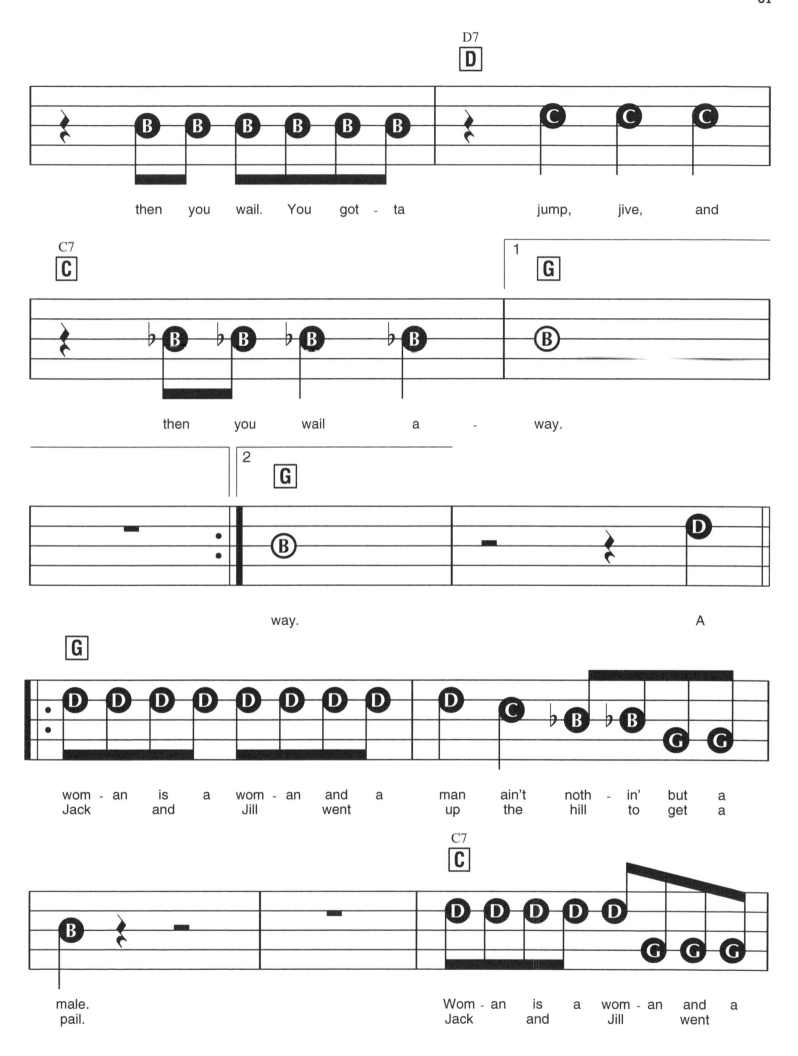

then you wail. You got - ta jump, jive, and

then you wail a - way.

way. A

wom - an is a wom - an and a man ain't noth - in' but a
Jack and Jill went up the hill to get a

male.
pail.

Wom - an is a wom - an and a
Jack and Jill went

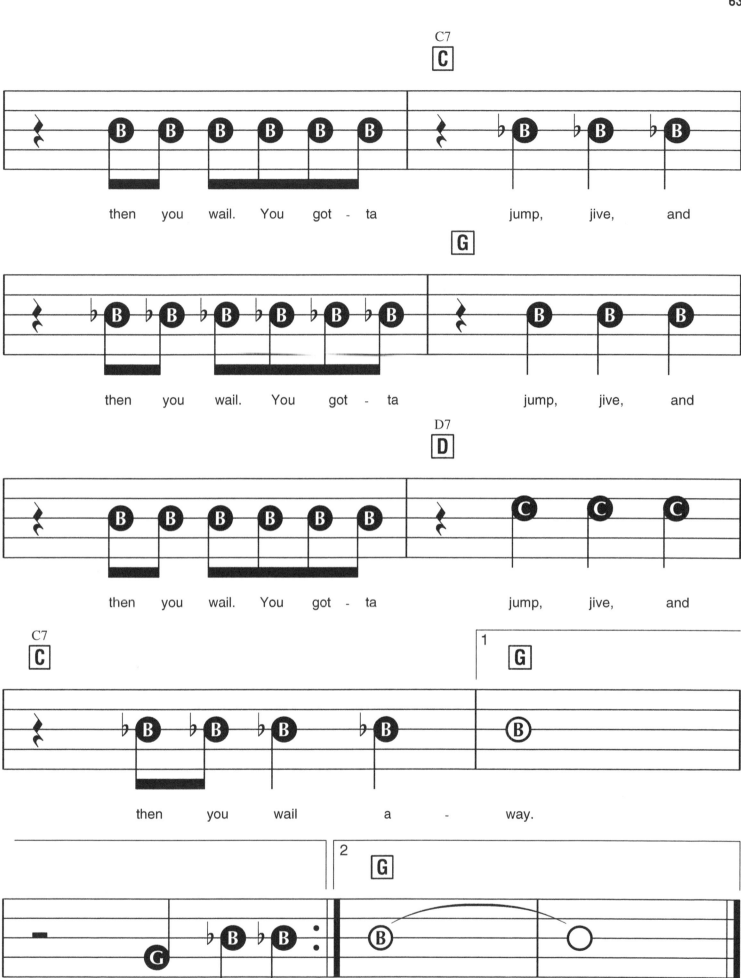

Limbo Rock

Registration 8
Rhythm: Rock or Calypso

Words and Music by Billy Strange
and Jon Sheldon

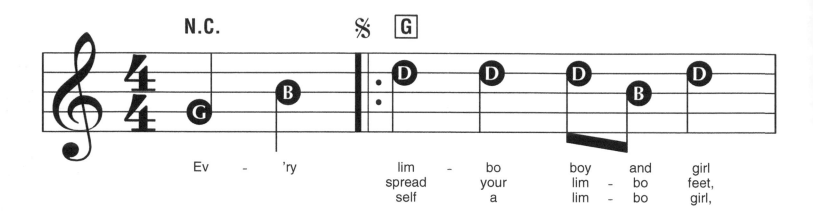

Ev - 'ry lim - bo boy and girl
spread your lim - bo feet,
self a lim - bo girl,

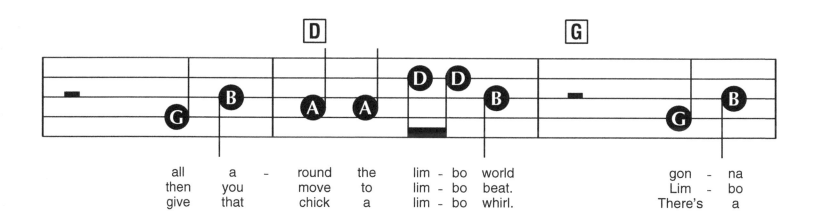

all a - round the lim - bo world gon - na
then you move to lim - bo beat. Lim - bo
give that chick a lim - bo whirl. There's a

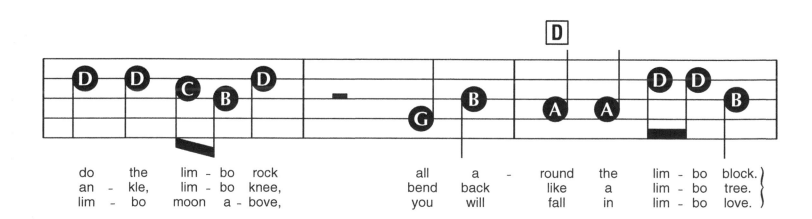

do the lim - bo rock all a - round the lim - bo block.
an - kle, lim - bo knee, bend back like a lim - bo tree.
lim - bo moon a - bove, you will fall in lim - bo love.

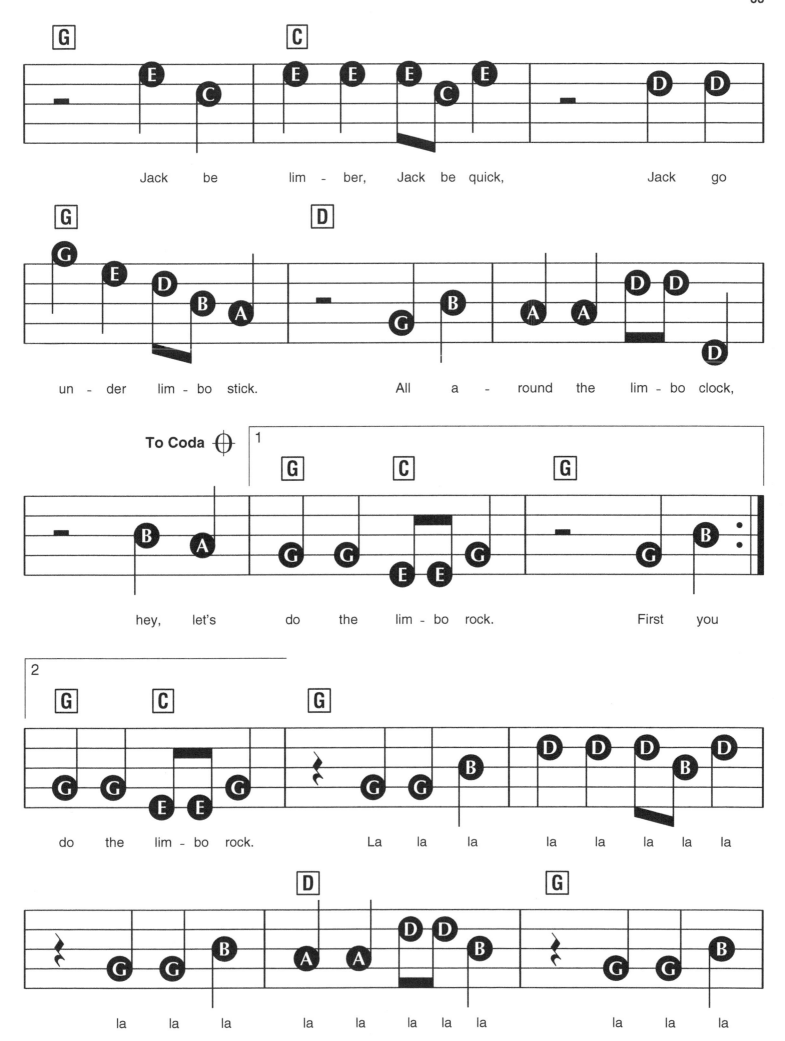

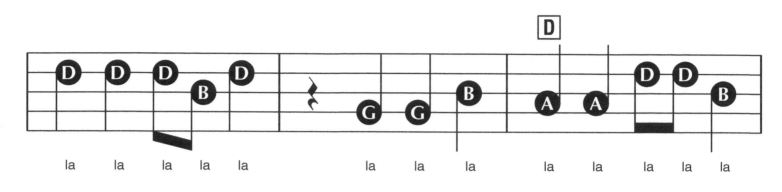

la la la la la   la la la   la la la la la

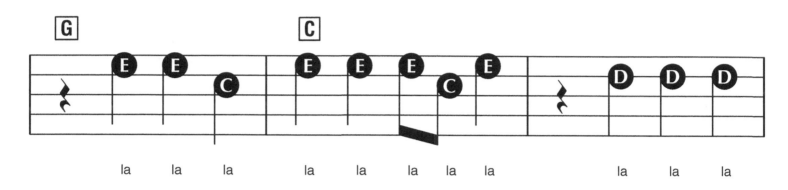

la la la   la la la la la   la la la

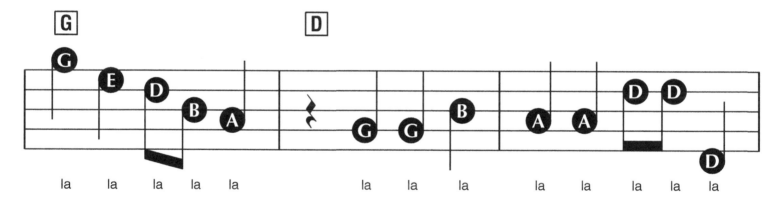

la la la la la   la la la   la la la la la

D.S. al Coda
(Return to %
Play to ⊕ and
Skip to Coda)

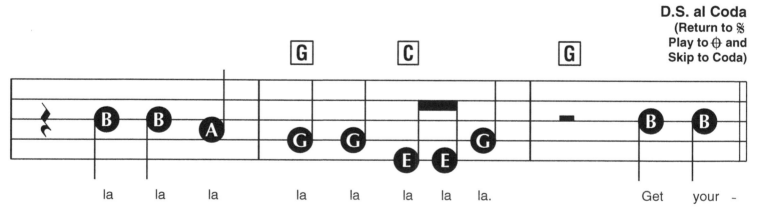

la la la   la la la la la.   Get your –

CODA

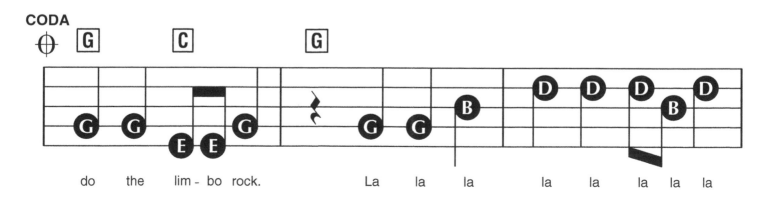

do the lim - bo rock.   La la la   la la la la la

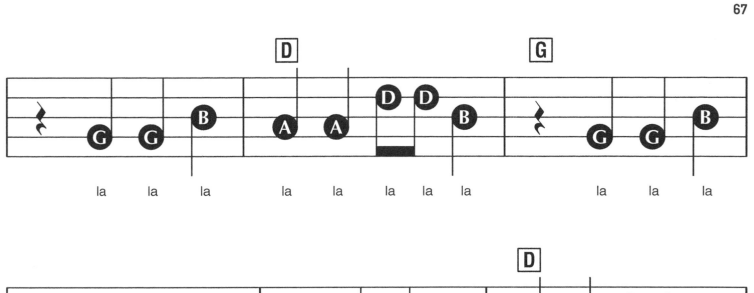

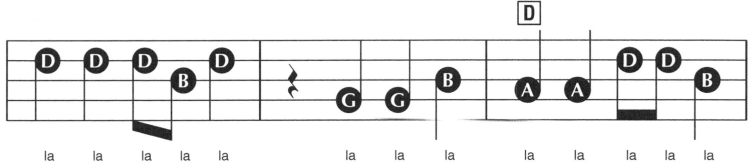

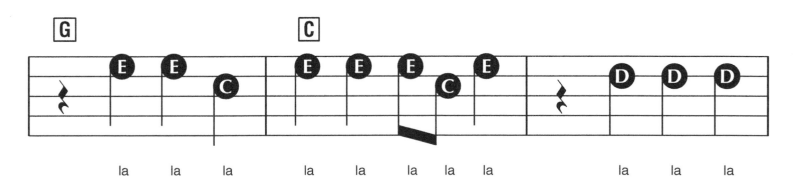

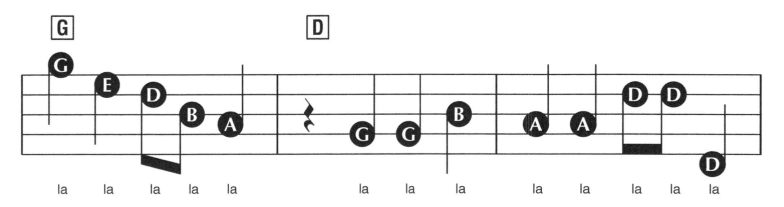

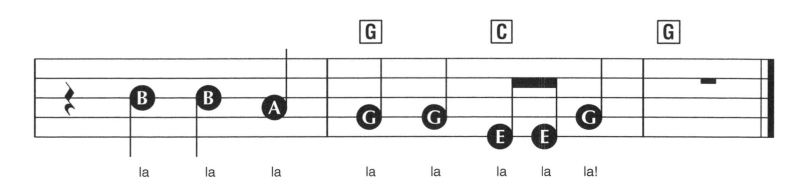

Livin' La Vida Loca

Registration 8
Rhythm: Latin or Latin Rock

Words and Music by Robi Rosa
and Desmond Child

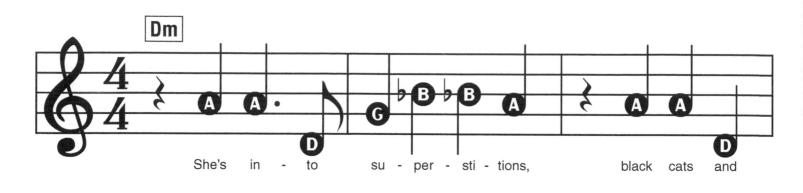

She's in - to su - per - sti - tions, black cats and

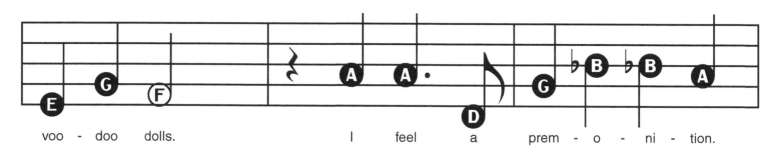

voo - doo dolls.   I feel   a   prem - o - ni - tion.

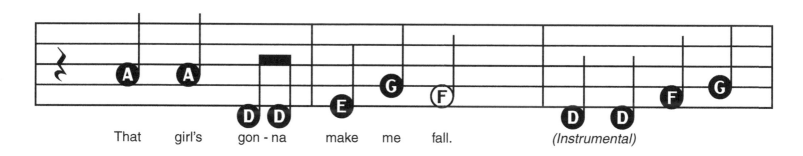

That girl's gon - na make me fall.   *(Instrumental)*

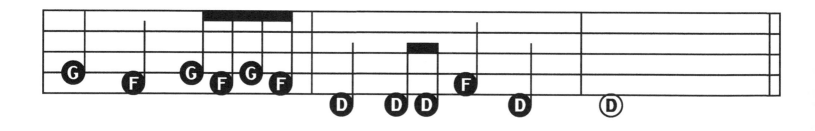

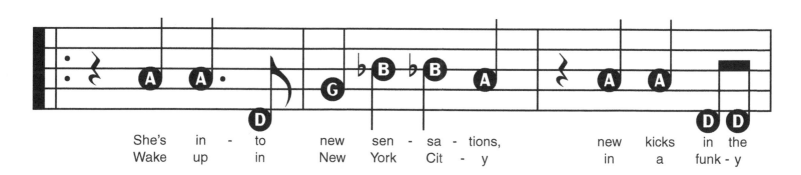

She's in - to new sen - sa - tions, new kicks in the
Wake up in New York Cit - y in a funk - y

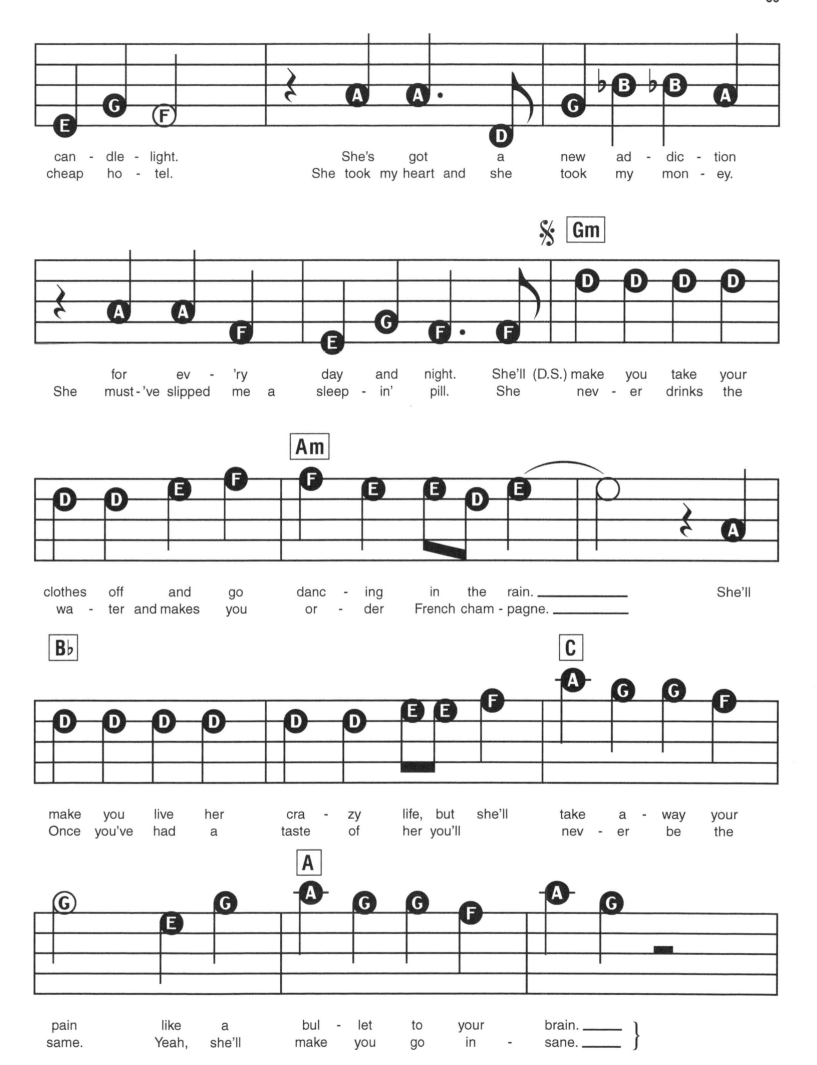

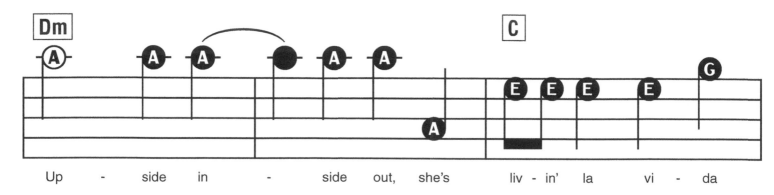

Up - side in - side out, she's liv - in' la vi - da

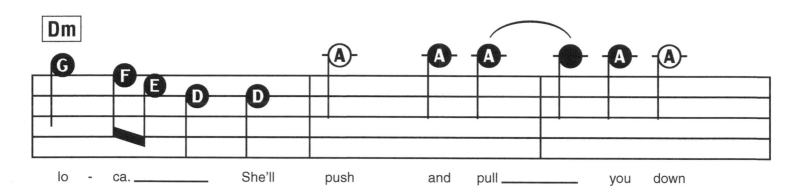

lo - ca. _____ She'll push and pull _____ you down

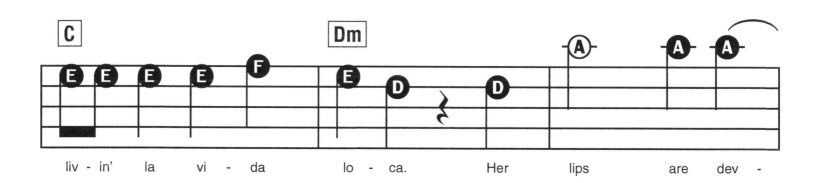

liv - in' la vi - da lo - ca. Her lips are dev -

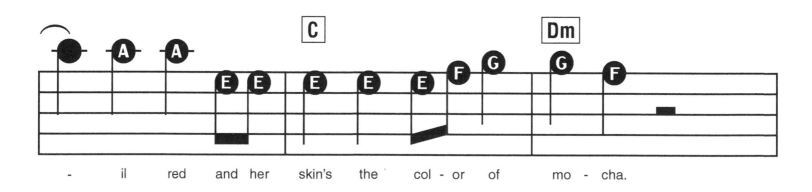

- il red and her skin's the col - or of mo - cha.

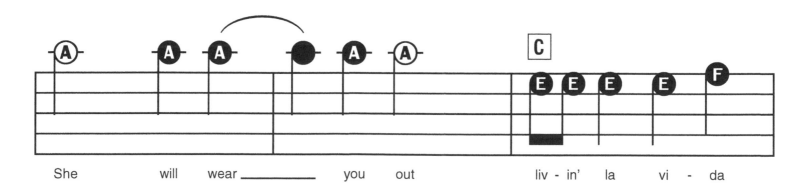

She will wear _____ you out liv - in' la vi - da

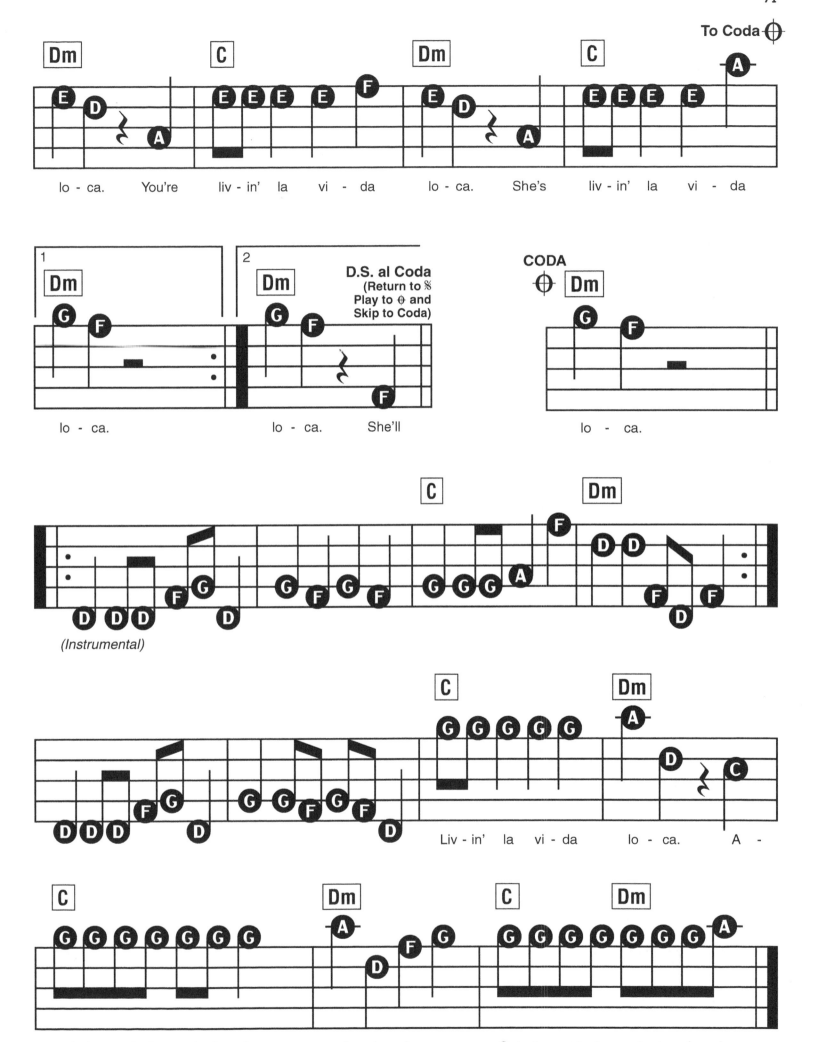

The Loco-Motion

Registration 4
Rhythm: Rock

Words and Music by Gerry Goffin
and Carole King

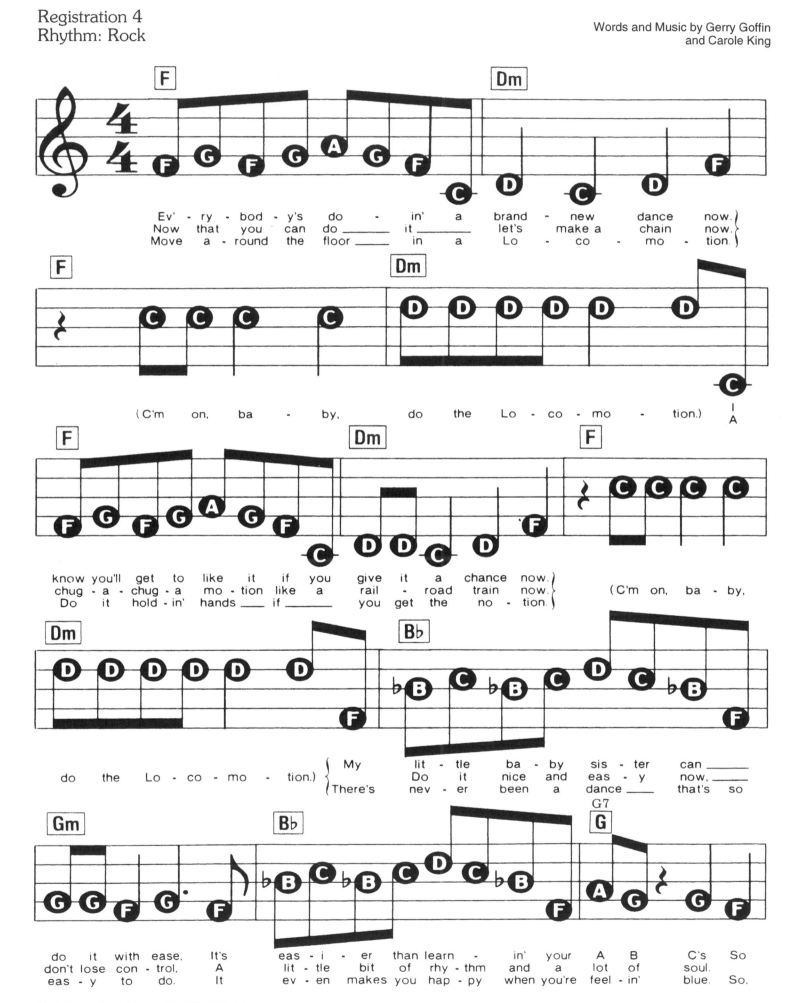

Ev' - ry - bod - y's do - in' a brand - new dance now.
Now that you can do _____ it _____ let's make a chain now.
Move a - round the floor _____ in a Lo - co - mo - tion.

(C'm on, ba - by, do the Lo - co - mo - tion.)

know you'll get to like it if you give it a chance now.
chug - a - chug - a mo - tion like a rail - road train now.
Do it hold - in' hands ____ if _____ you get the no - tion.

(C'm on, ba - by,

do the Lo - co - mo - tion.)   My lit - tle ba - by sis - ter can _____
Do it nice and eas - y now, _____
There's nev - er been a dance ____ that's so

do it with ease. It's eas - i - er than learn - in' your A B C's So
don't lose con - trol. A lit - tle bit of rhy - thm and a lot of soul.
eas - y to do. It ev - en makes you hap - py when you're feel - in' blue. So.

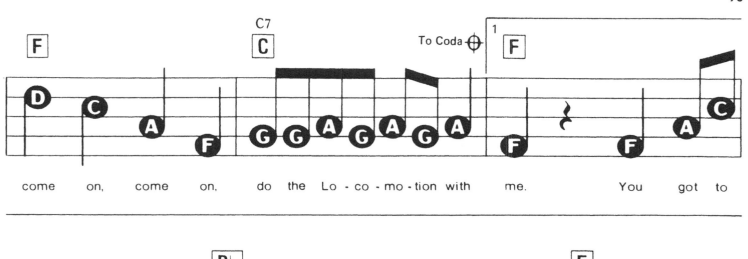

come on, come on, do the Lo - co - mo - tion with me. You got to

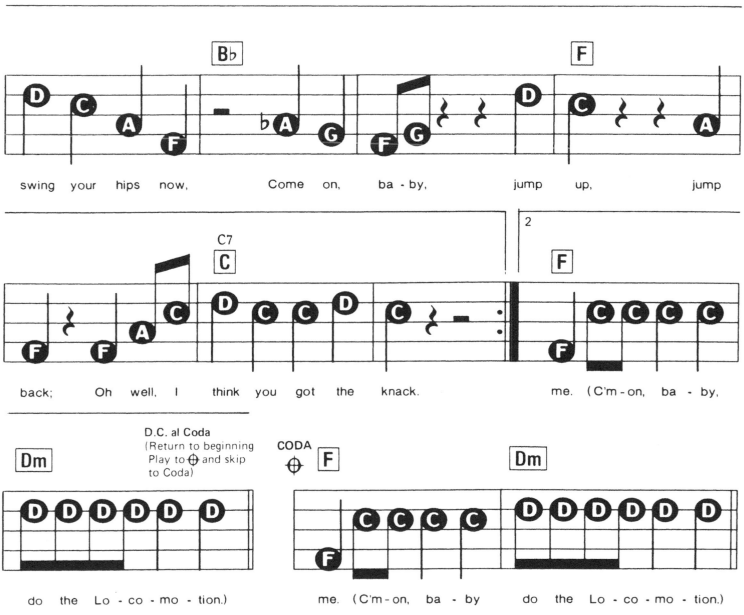

swing your hips now, Come on, ba - by, jump up, jump

back; Oh well, I think you got the knack. me. (C'm - on, ba - by,

D.C. al Coda
(Return to beginning
Play to ⊕ and skip
to Coda)

CODA

do the Lo - co - mo - tion.) me. (C'm - on, ba - by do the Lo - co - mo - tion.)

Repeat and Fade

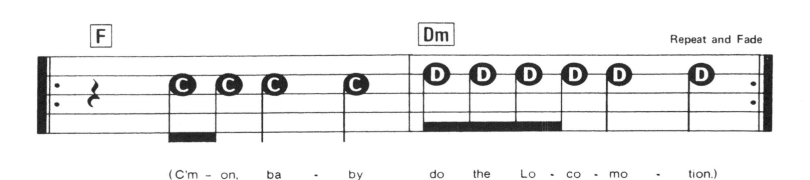

(C'm - on, ba - by do the Lo - co - mo - tion.)

Louie, Louie

Registration 5
Rhythm: Rock

Words and Music by
Richard Berry

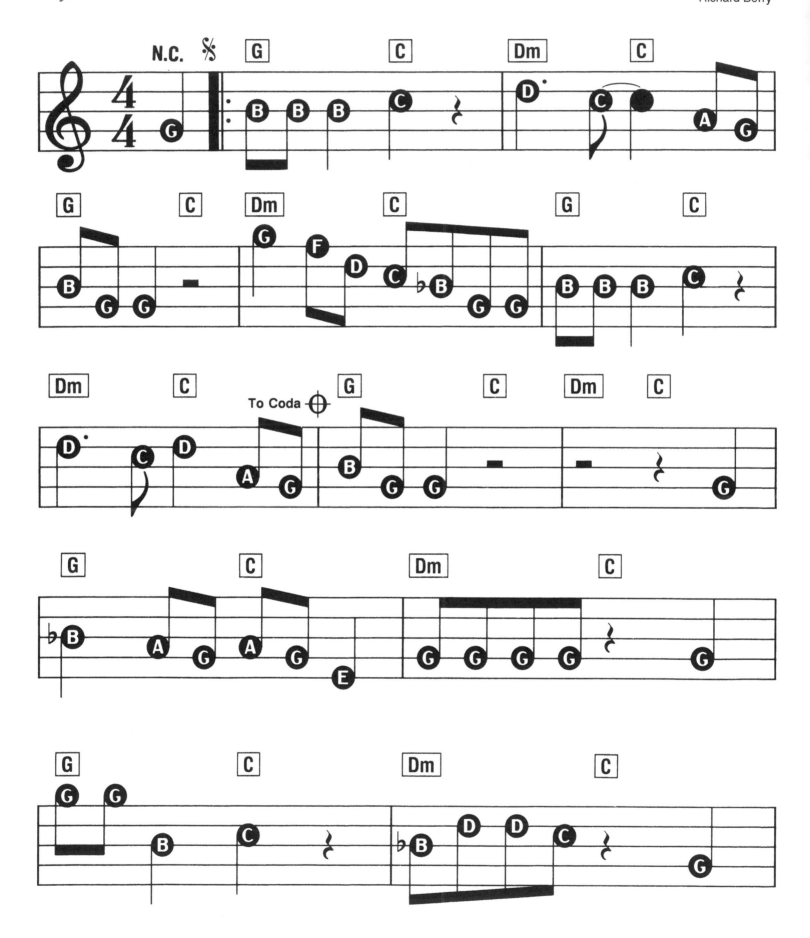

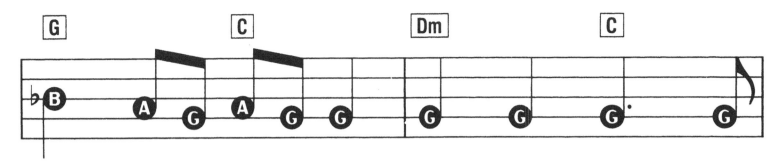

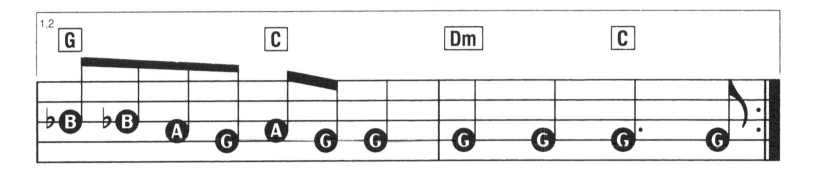

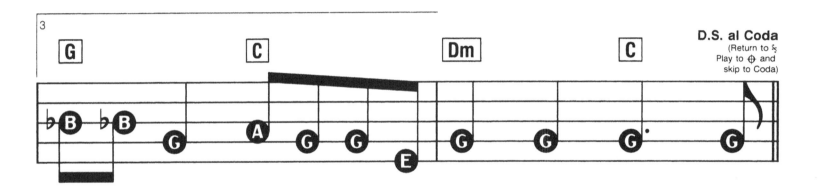

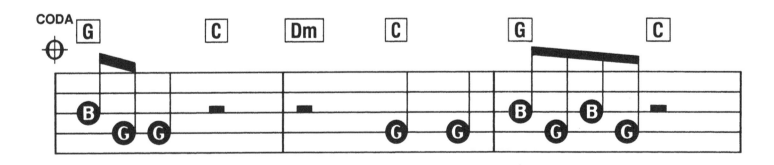

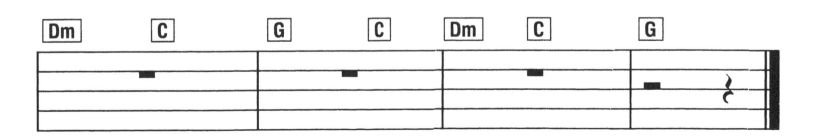

La Bamba

Registration 4
Rhythm: Latin

By Ritchie Valens

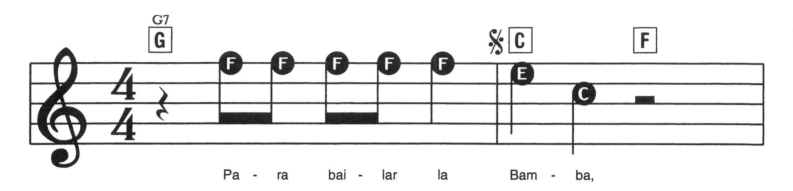

Pa - ra bai - lar la Bam - ba,

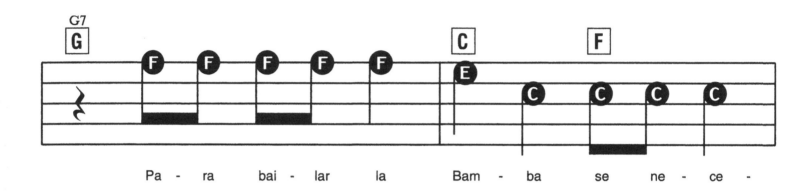

Pa - ra bai - lar la Bam - ba se ne - ce -

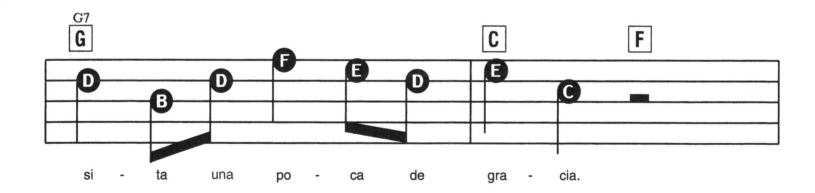

si - ta una po - ca de gra - cia.

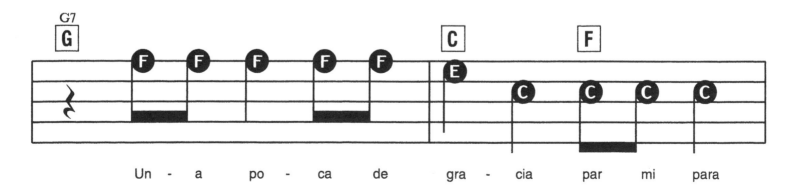

Un - a po - ca de gra - cia par mi para

77

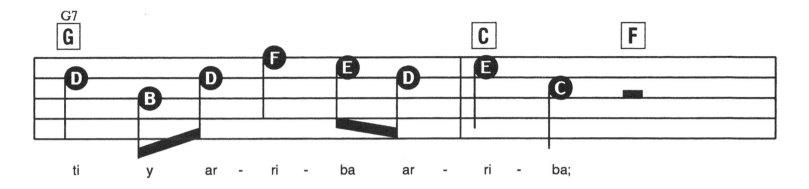

ti y ar - ri - ba ar - ri - ba;

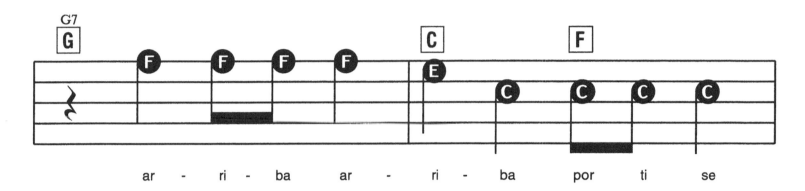

ar - ri - ba ar - ri - ba por ti se

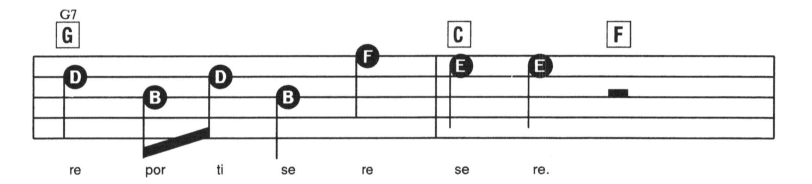

re por ti se re se re.

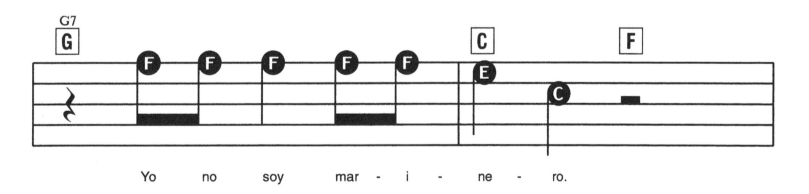

Yo no soy mar - i - ne - ro.

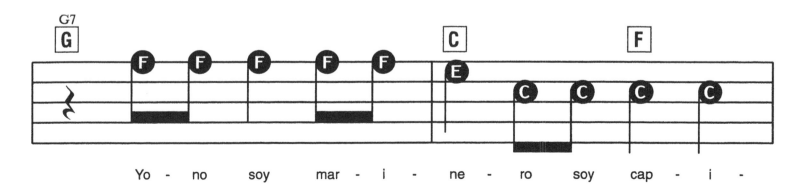

Yo no soy mar - i - ne - ro soy cap - i -

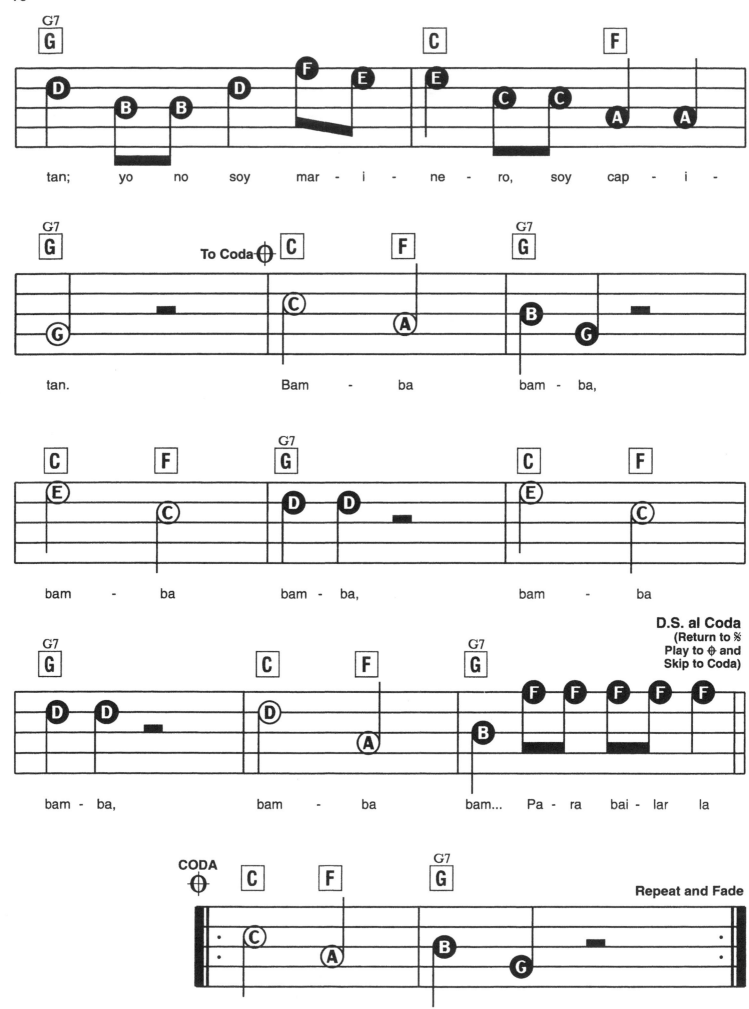

Macho Man

Registration 7
Rhythm: Disco or Rock

Words and Music by Jacques Morali,
Henri Belolo, Victor Willis
and Peter Whitehead

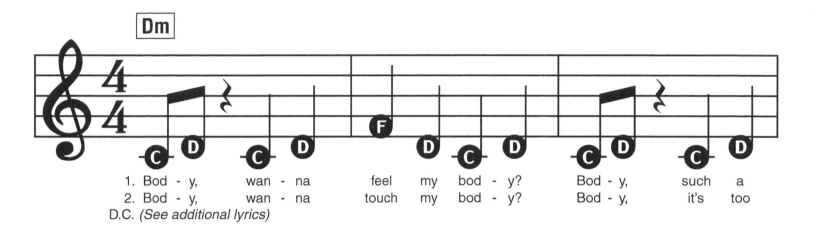

1. Bod - y, wan - na feel my bod - y? Bod - y, such a
2. Bod - y, wan - na touch my bod - y? Bod - y, it's too

D.C. *(See additional lyrics)*

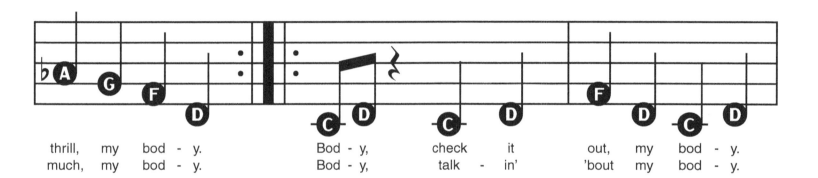

thrill, my bod - y. Bod - y, check it out, my bod - y.
much, my bod - y. Bod - y, talk - in' 'bout my bod - y.

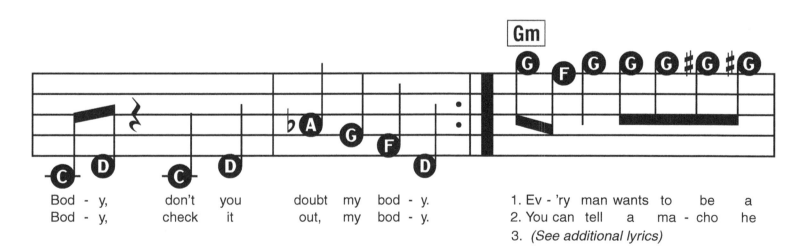

Bod - y, don't you doubt my bod - y.
Bod - y, check it out, my bod - y.

1. Ev - 'ry man wants to be a
2. You can tell a ma - cho he
3. *(See additional lyrics)*

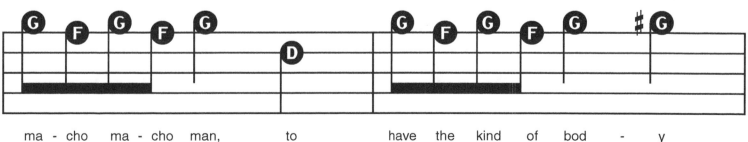

ma - cho ma - cho man, to have the kind of bod - y
has a funk - y walk his west - ern shirts and leath - er

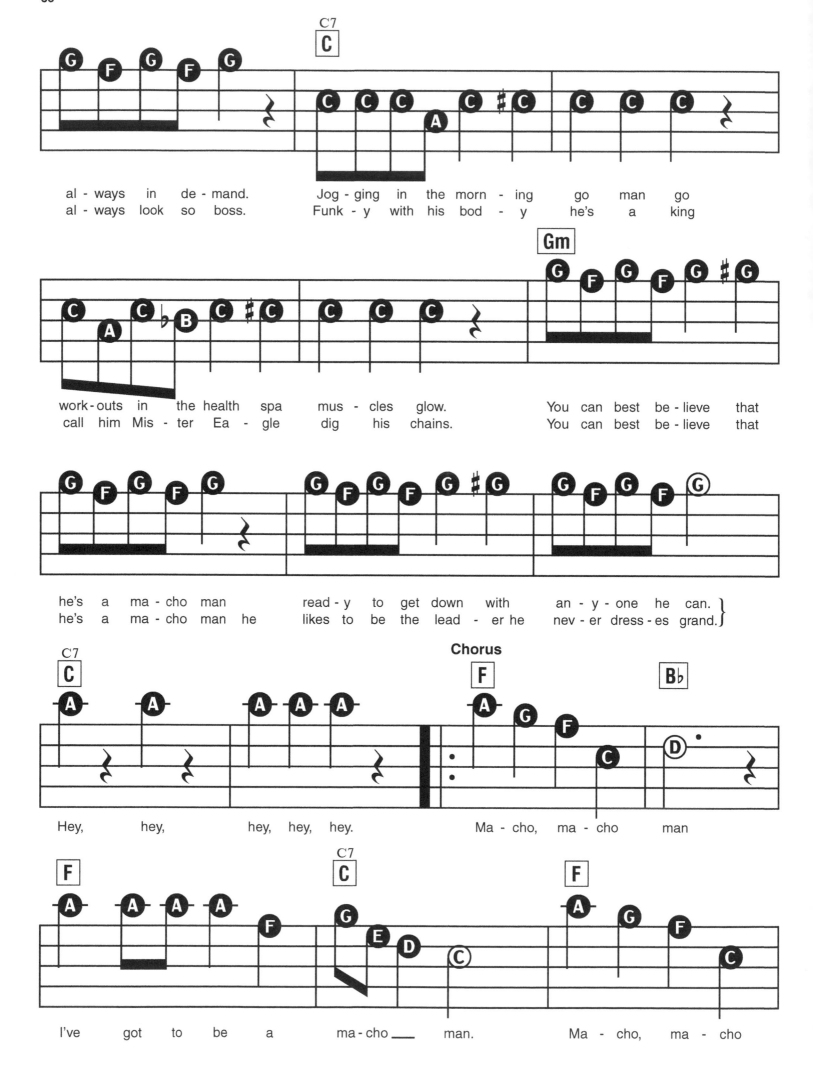

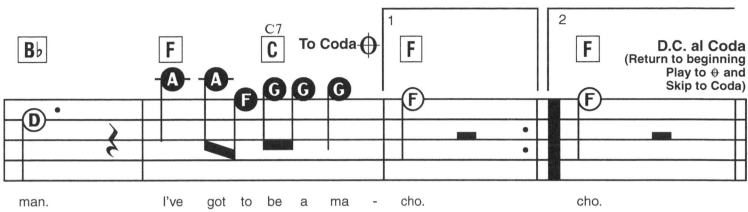

man.   I've got to be a ma - cho.   cho.

CODA

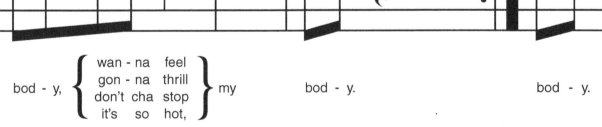

cho.   Bod - y,   bod - y,

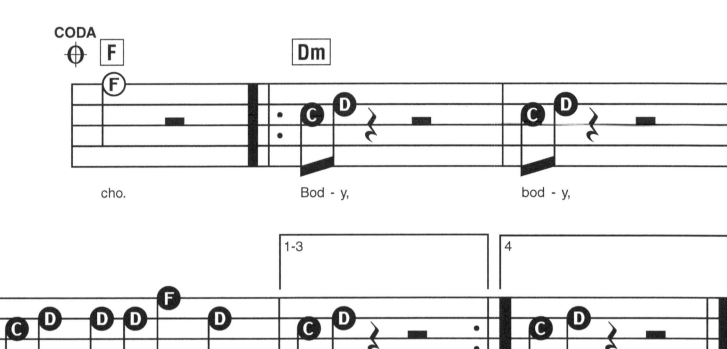

bod - y,
{
wan - na feel
gon - na thrill
don't cha stop
it's so hot,
} my   bod - y.   bod - y.

Additional Lyrics

D.C.   Body, it's so hot, my body,
         Body, love to pop my body.
         Body, love to please my body.
         Body, don't you tease my body.
         Body, you'll adore my body.
         Body, come explore my body.
         Body, made by God, my body.
         Body, it's so good, my body.

3. Ev'ry man ought to be a macho man.
    To live a life of freedom machos make a stand.
    Have their own life style and ideals.
    Possess the strength and confidence life's a steal.
    You can best believe that he's a macho man.
    He's a special person in anybody's land.
    Chorus

Mambo No. 5
(A Little Bit Of...)

Registration 4
Rhythm: 8 Beat or Rock

Original Music by Damaso Perez Prado
Words by Lou Bega and Zippy

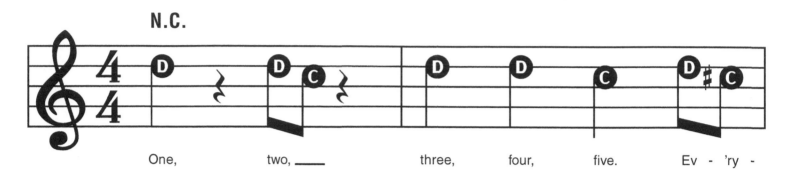

One, two, _____ three, four, five. Ev - 'ry -

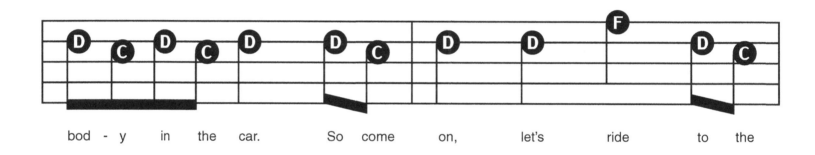

bod - y in the car. So come on, let's ride to the

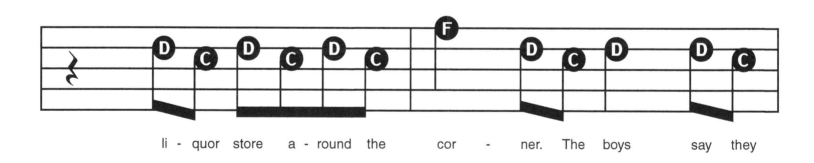

li - quor store a - round the cor - ner. The boys say they

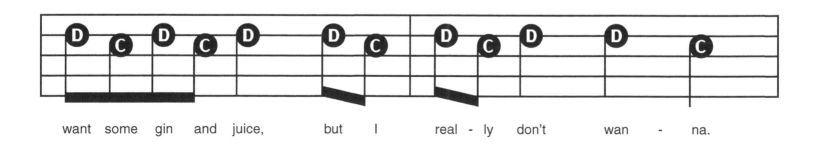

want some gin and juice, but I real - ly don't wan - na.

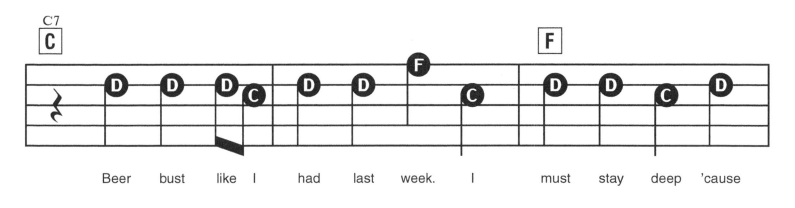

Beer bust like I had last week. I must stay deep 'cause

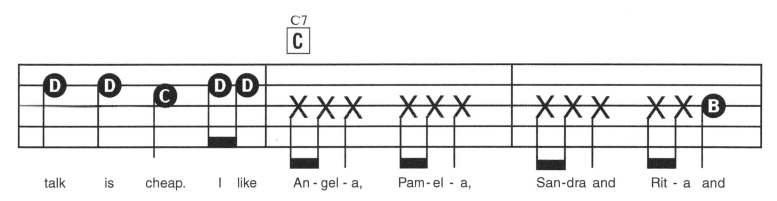

talk is cheap. I like An - gel - a, Pam- el - a, San-dra and Rit - a and

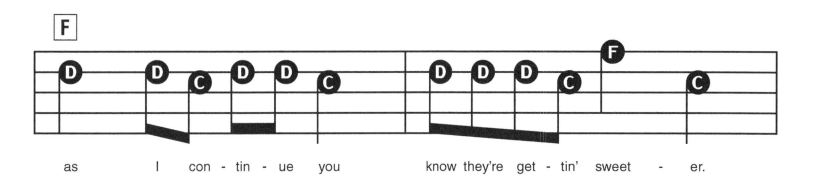

as I con - tin - ue you know they're get - tin' sweet - er.

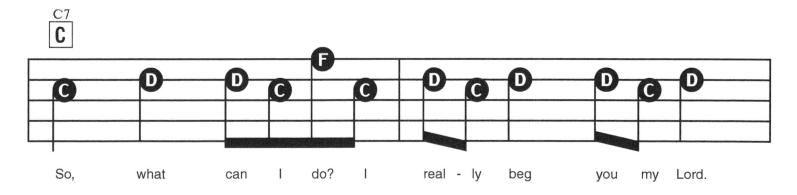

So, what can I do? I real - ly beg you my Lord.

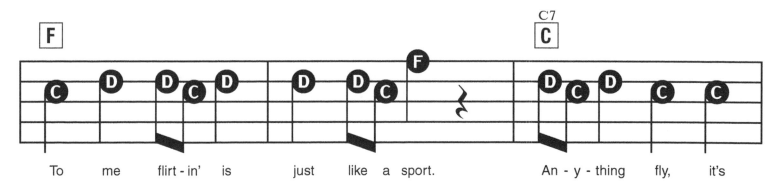

To me flirt-in' is just like a sport. An - y - thing fly, it's

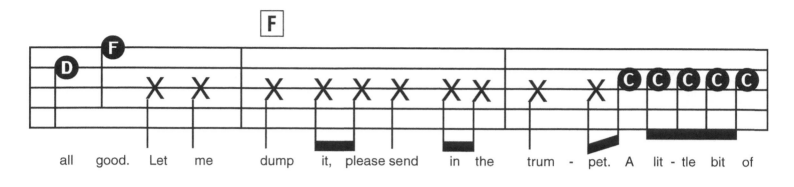

all good. Let me dump it, please send in the trum - pet. A lit - tle bit of

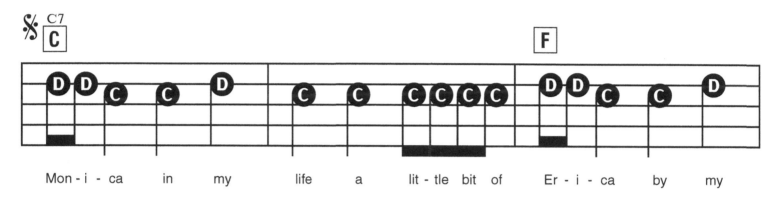

Mon - i - ca in my life a lit - tle bit of Er - i - ca by my

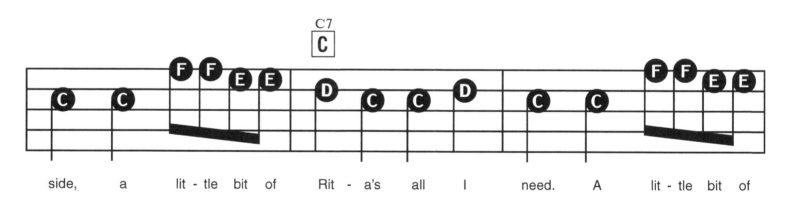

side, a lit - tle bit of Rit - a's all I need. A lit - tle bit of

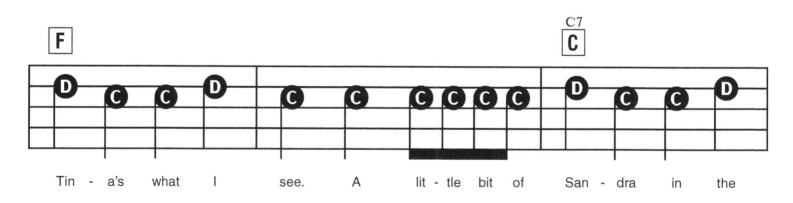

Tin - a's what I see. A lit - tle bit of San - dra in the

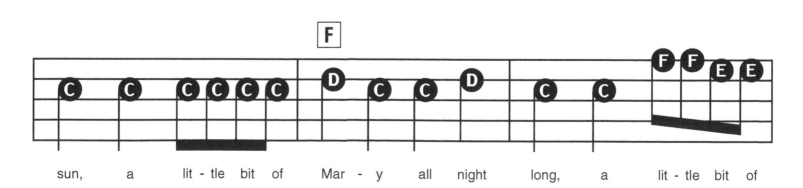

sun, a lit - tle bit of Mar - y all night long, a lit - tle bit of

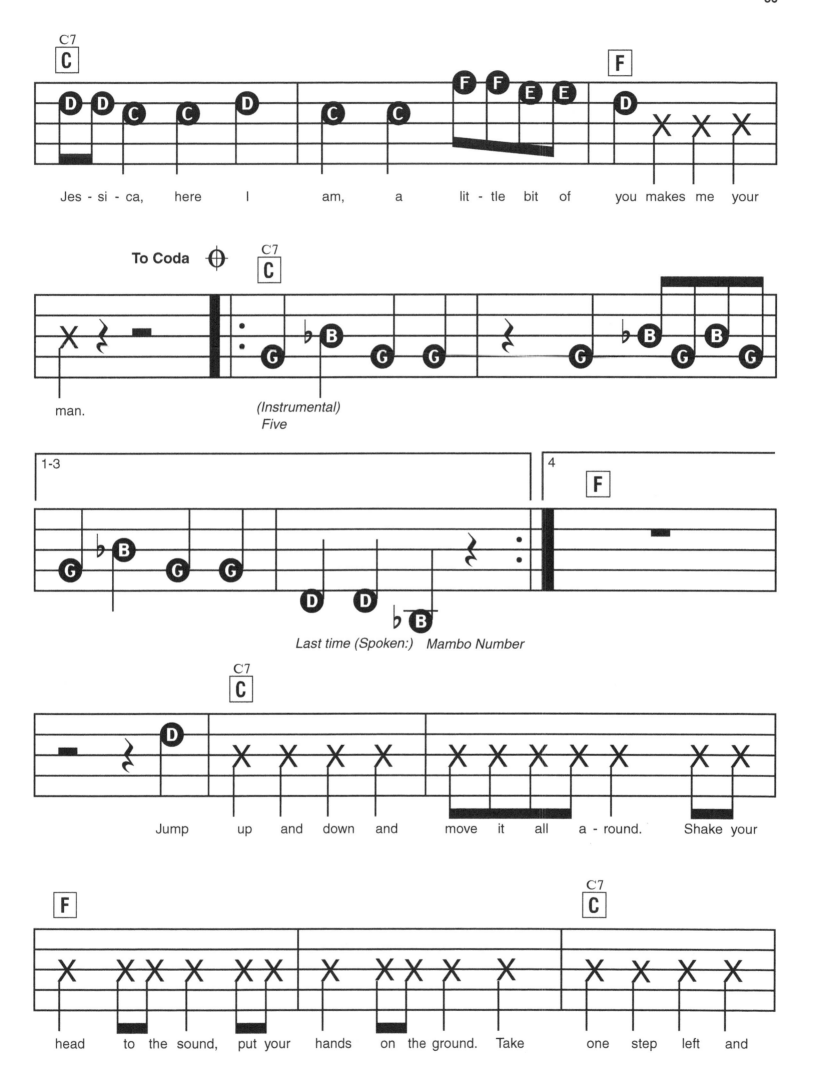

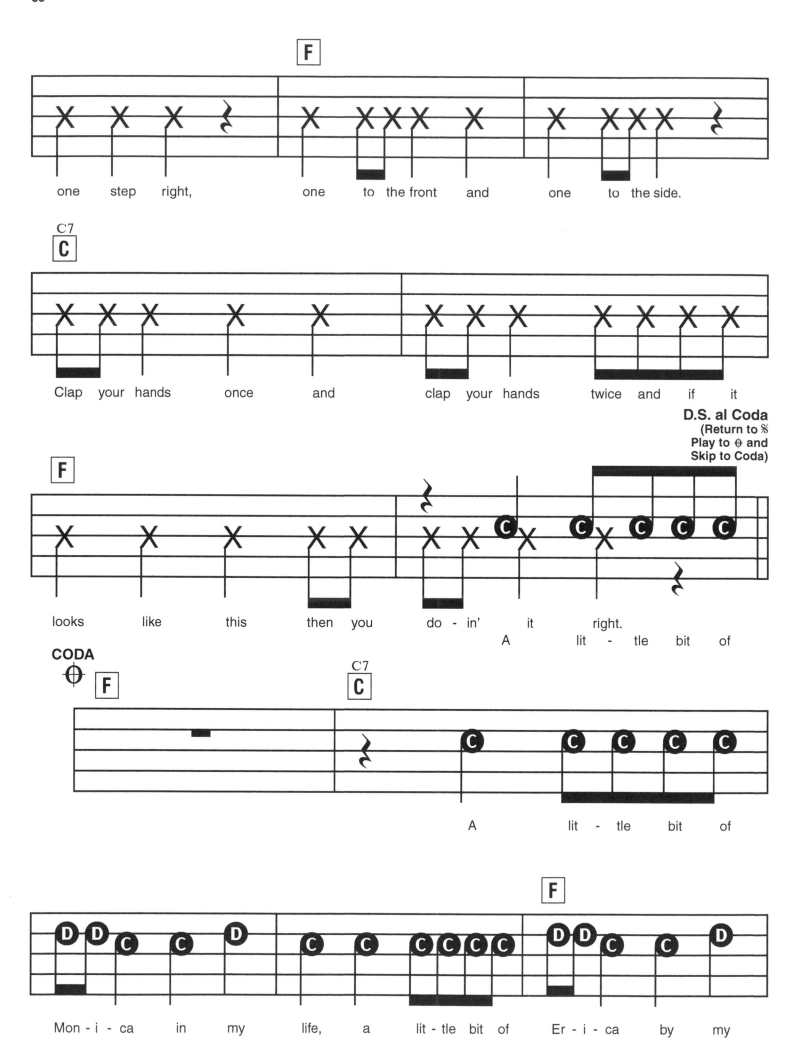

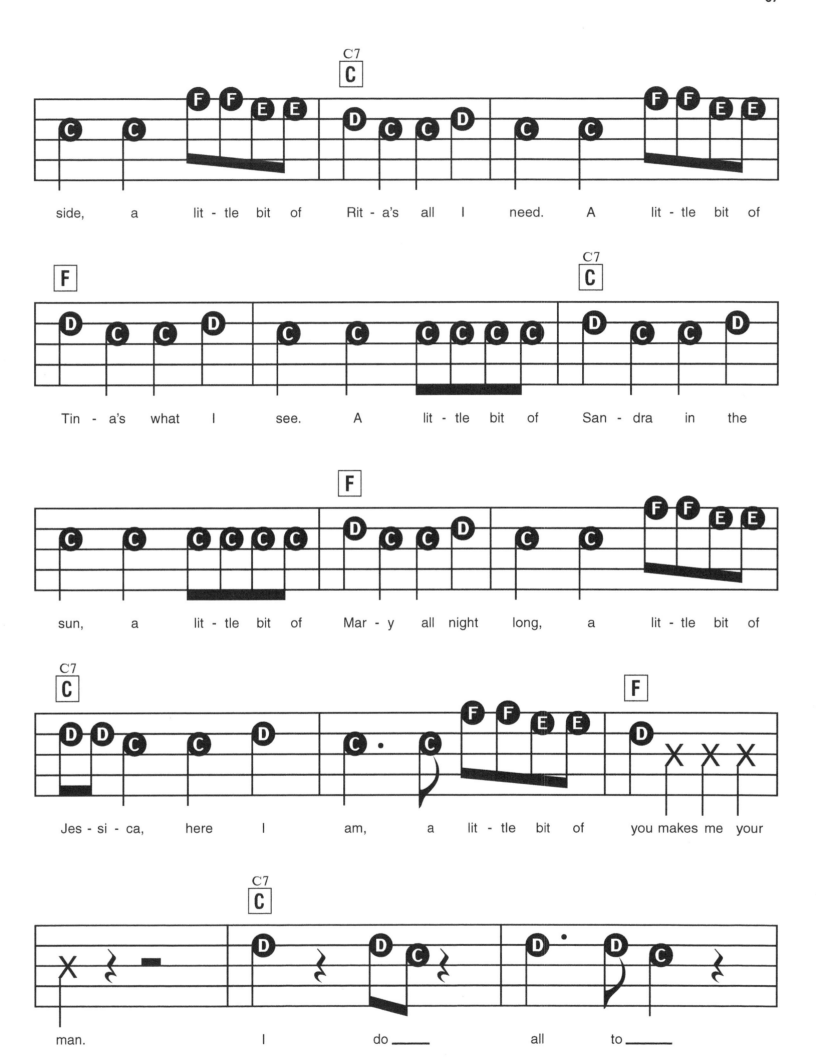

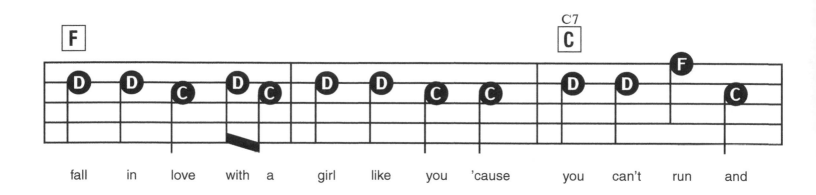

fall   in   love   with   a   girl   like   you   'cause   you   can't   run   and

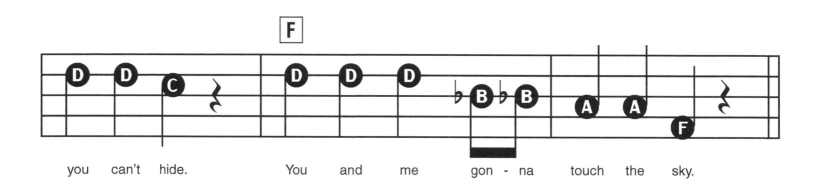

you   can't   hide.   You   and   me   gon - na   touch   the   sky.

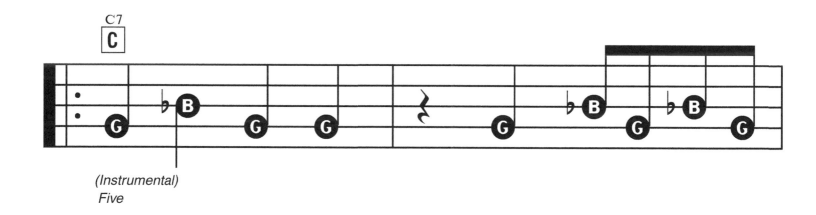

(Instrumental)
Five

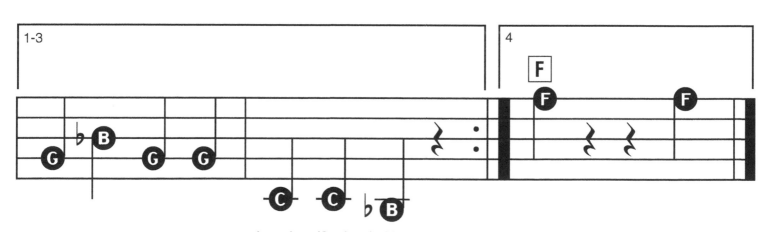

Last time (Spoken:) Mambo Number

Mony, Mony

Registration 8
Rhythm: Rock

Words and Music by Bobby Bloom,
Tommy James, Ritchie Cordell
and Bo Gentry

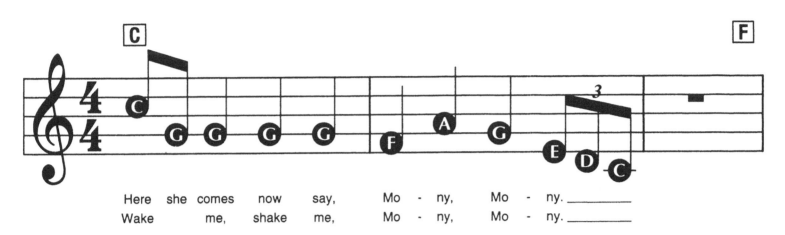

Here she comes now say, Mo - ny, Mo - ny. _____
Wake me, shake me, Mo - ny, Mo - ny. _____

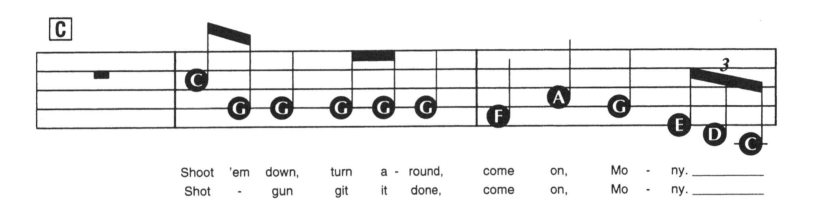

Shoot 'em down, turn a - round, come on, Mo - ny. _____
Shot - gun git it done, come on, Mo - ny. _____

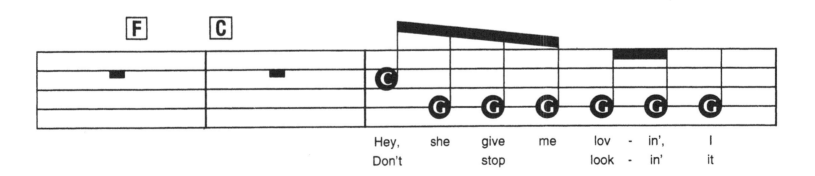

Hey, she give me lov - in', I
Don't stop look - in' it

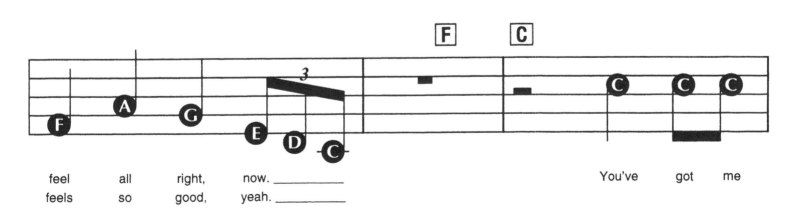

feel all right, now. _____
feels so good, yeah. _____

You've got me

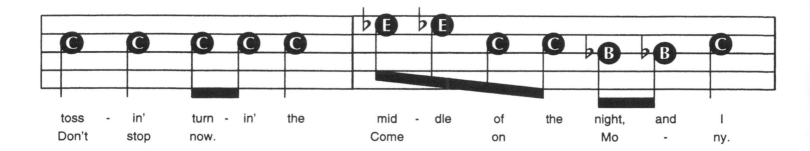

toss - in' turn - in' the mid - dle of the night, and I
Don't stop now. Come on Mo - ny.

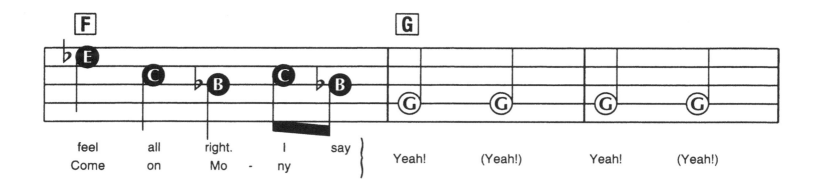

feel all right. I say
Come on Mo - ny
Yeah! (Yeah!) Yeah! (Yeah!)

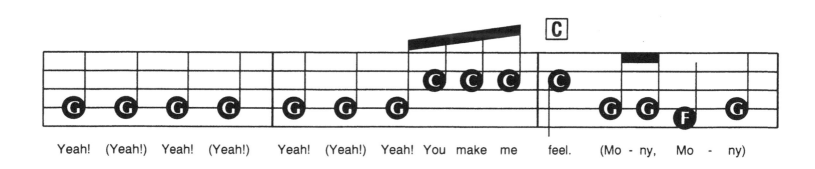

Yeah! (Yeah!) Yeah! (Yeah!) Yeah! (Yeah!) Yeah! You make me feel. (Mo - ny, Mo - ny)

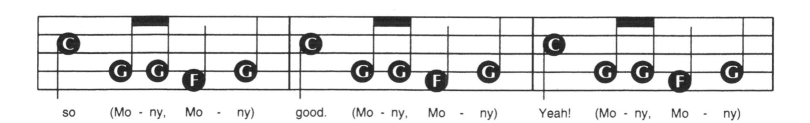

so (Mo - ny, Mo - ny) good. (Mo - ny, Mo - ny) Yeah! (Mo - ny, Mo - ny)

Yeah! (Mo - ny, Mo - ny) Yeah! (Mo - ny, Mo - ny) Yeah! (Mo - ny, Mo - ny)

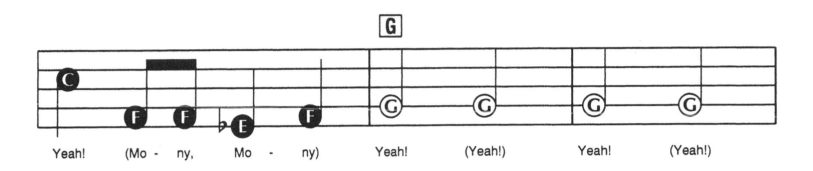

Yeah! (Mo - ny, Mo - ny) Yeah! (Yeah!) Yeah! (Yeah!)

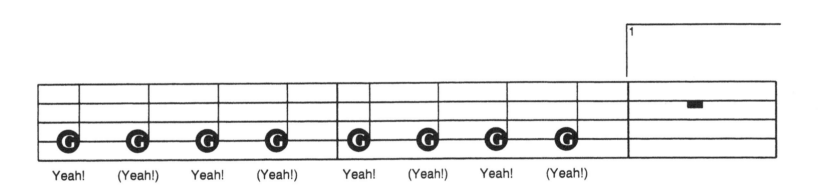

Yeah! (Yeah!) Yeah! (Yeah!) Yeah! (Yeah!) Yeah! (Yeah!)

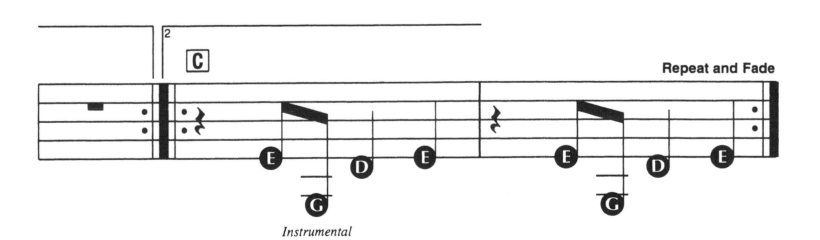

Repeat and Fade

Instrumental

Monster Mash

Registration 8
Rhythm: Rock

Words and Music by Bobby Pickett
and Leonard Capizzi

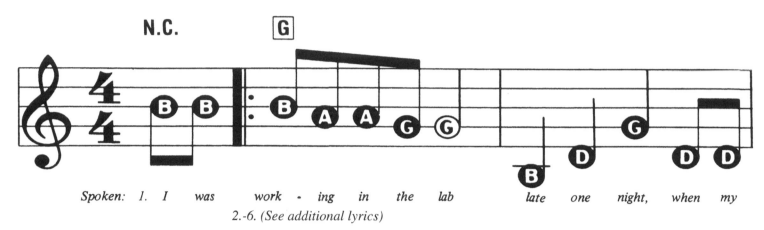

Spoken: 1. I was work - ing in the lab late one night, when my
2.-6. (See additional lyrics)

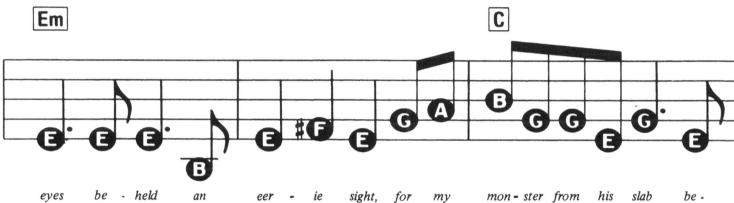

eyes be - held an eer - ie sight, for my mon - ster from his slab be -

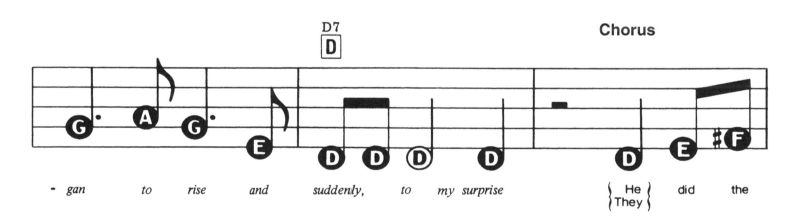

- gan to rise and suddenly, to my surprise { He / They } did the

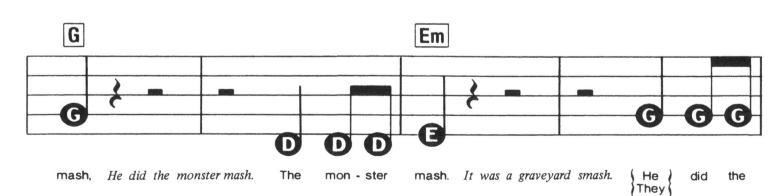

mash, *He did the monster mash.* The mon - ster mash. *It was a graveyard smash.* { He / They } did the

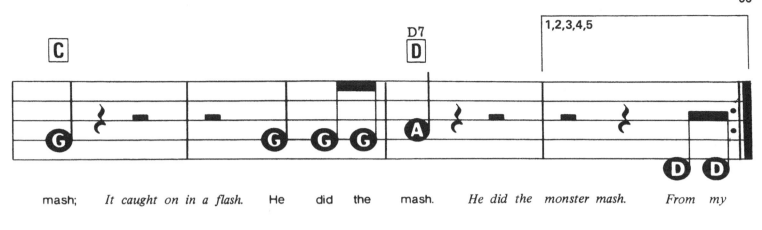

mash;   *It caught on in a flash.*   He   did   the   mash.   *He did the monster mash.*   *From my*

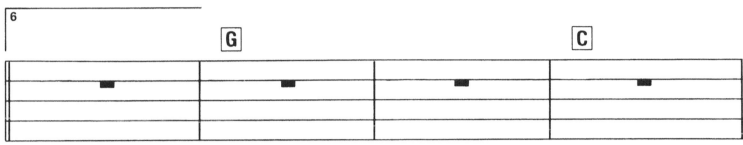

monster mash   *Spoken: Mash good,*   *easy,*   *Igor, you impetuous*

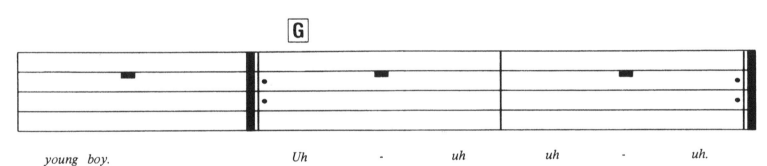

young boy.   *Uh - uh uh - uh.*

Additional lyrics

2. *From my laboratory in the castle east.*
   To the master bedroom where the vampires feast.
   The ghouls all came from their humble abodes
   To catch a jolt from my electrodes.
   (to Chorus: They did the mash)

3. *The zombies were having fun,*
   The party had just begun.
   The guests included Wolf-man,
   Dracula, and his son.

4. *The scene was rockin'; all were digging the sounds,*
   Igor on chains, backed by his baying hounds.
   The coffin-bangers were about to arrive
   With their vocal group "The Crypt-Kicker Five"
   (to Chorus: They played the mash)

5. *Out from his coffin, Drac's voice did ring;*
   Seems he was troubled by just one thing.
   He opened the lid and shook his fist,
   And said, "Whatever happened to my Transylvanian twist?"
   (to Chorus: It's now the mash)

6. *Now everything's cool, Drac's a part of the band*
   And my monster mash is the hit of the land.
   For you, the living, this mash was meant too,
   When you get to my door, tell them Boris sent you. (till fade)
   (to Chorus: And you can mash)

Yellow Submarine

Registration 2
Rhythm: 8 Beat or Rock

Words and Music by John Lennon
and Paul McCartney

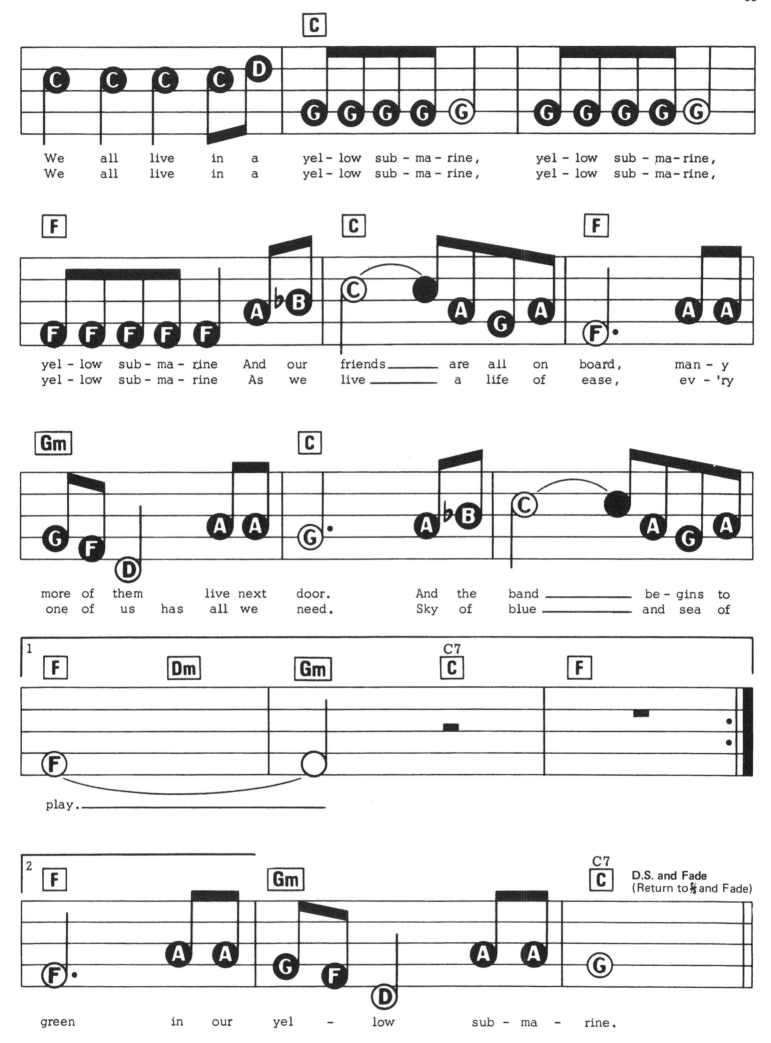

Rock & Roll - Part II
(The Hey Song)

Registration 4
Rhythm: Rock 'n' Roll or Rock

Words and Music by Mike Leander
and Gary Glitter

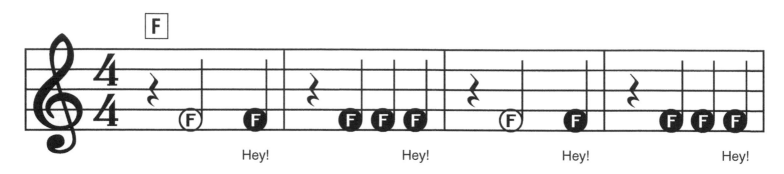

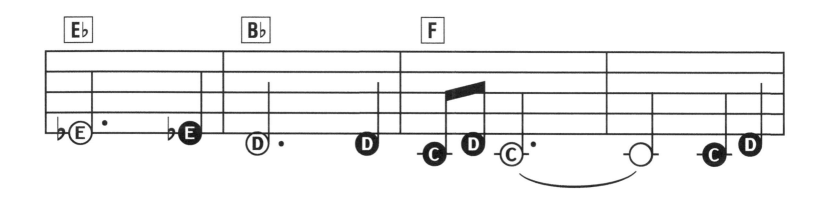

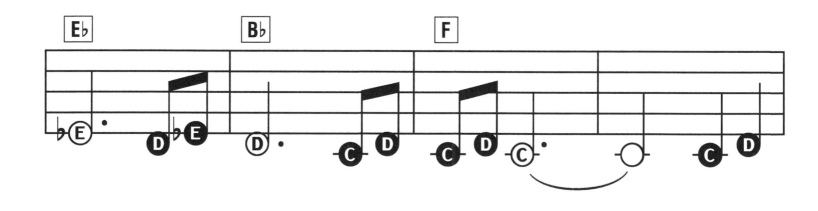

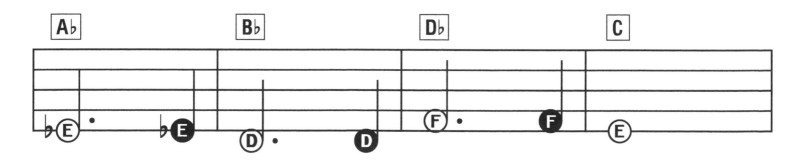

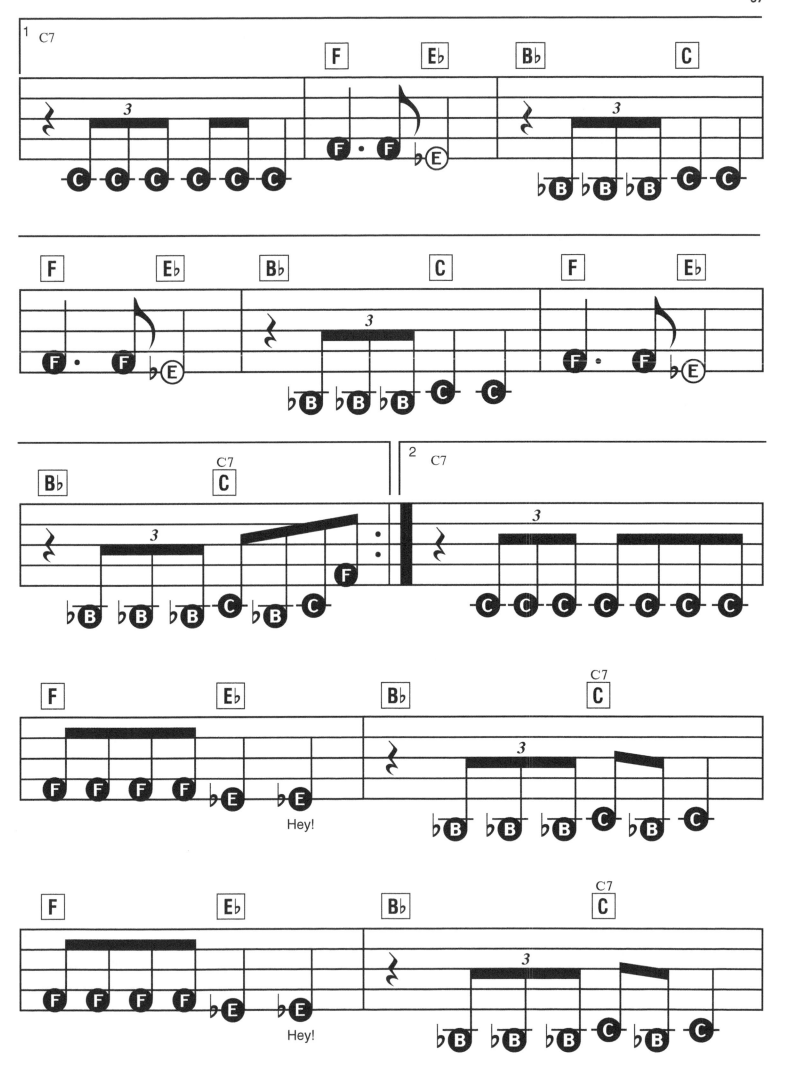

98

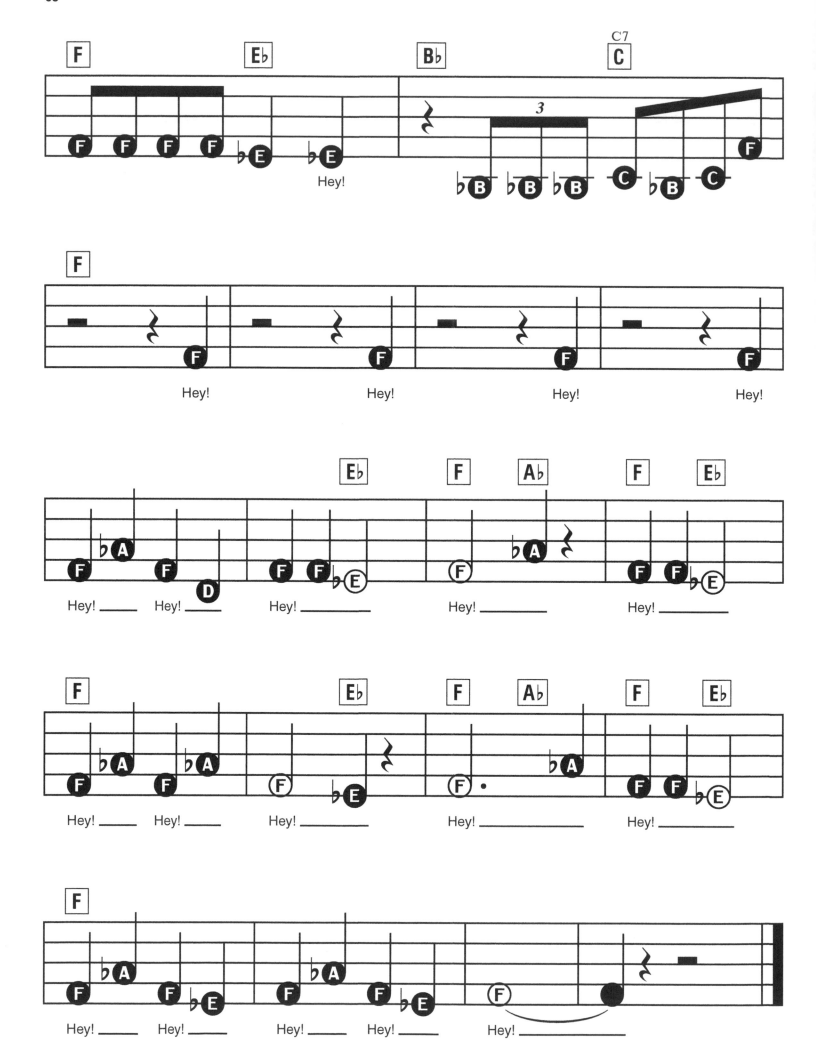

Rock and Roll All Nite

Registration 8
Rhythm: Rock 'n' Roll or Rock

Words and Music by Paul Stanley
and Gene Simmons

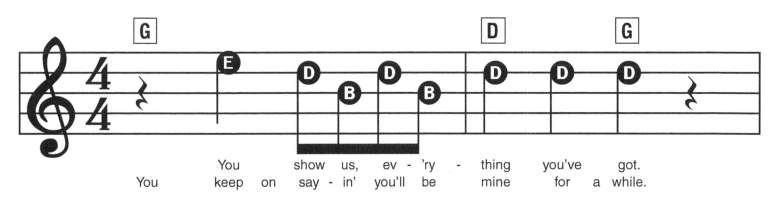

You   show us, ev - 'ry - thing you've got.
You   keep on say - in' you'll be   mine   for a while.

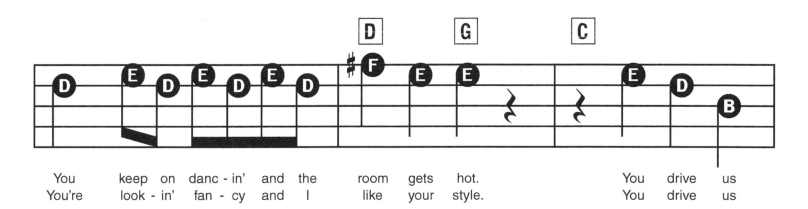

You   keep on danc - in' and the   room   gets hot.   You   drive us
You're   look - in' fan - cy and I   like your style.   You   drive us

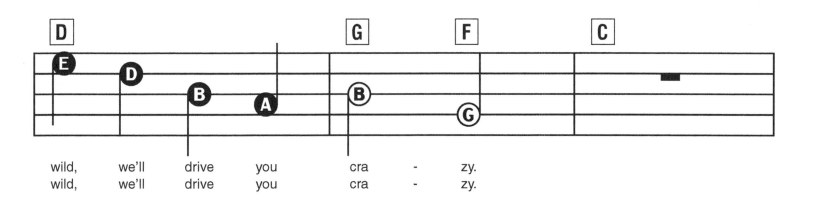

wild,   we'll   drive   you   cra - zy.
wild,   we'll   drive   you   cra - zy.

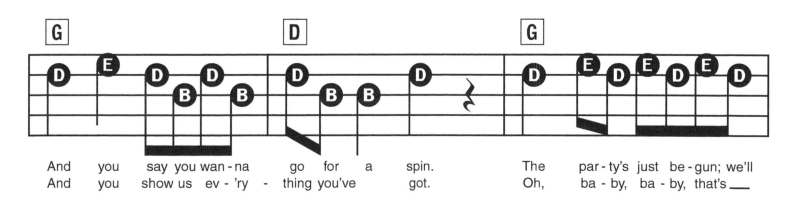

And   you   say you wan - na   go   for a   spin.   The   par - ty's just be - gun; we'll
And   you   show us ev - 'ry - thing you've   got.   Oh,   ba - by, ba - by, that's ___

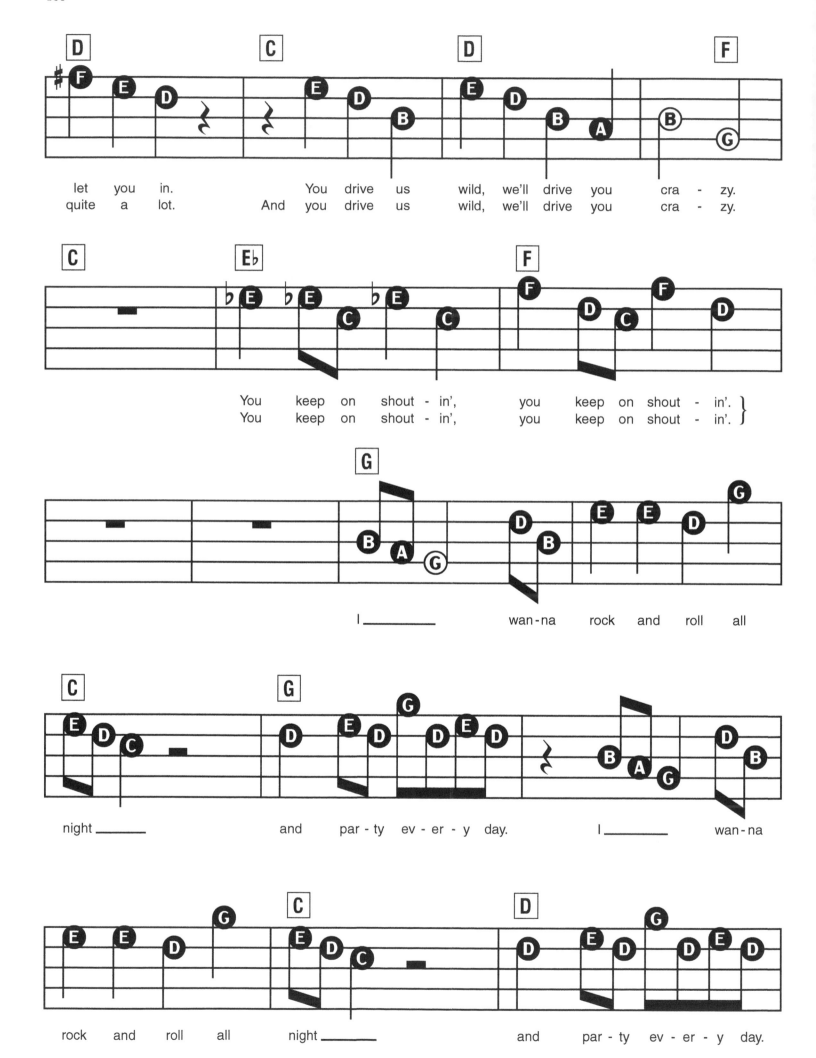

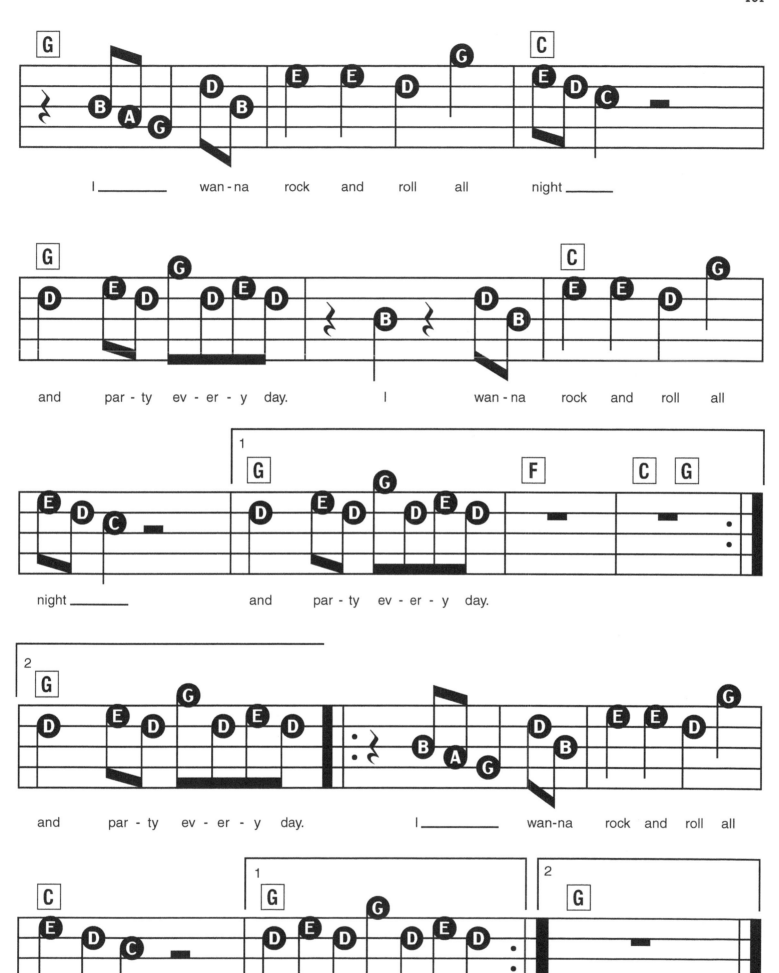

Shout

Registration 4
Rhythm: Dance or Rock

Words and Music by O'Kelly Isley,
Ronald Isley and Rudolph Isley

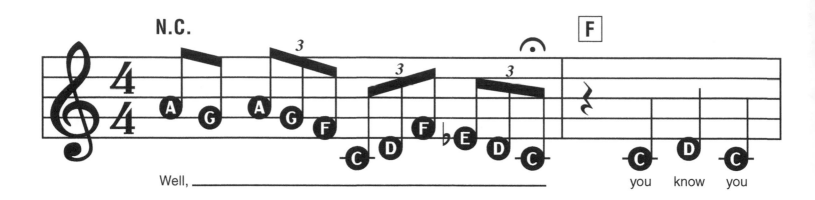

Well, _____ you know you

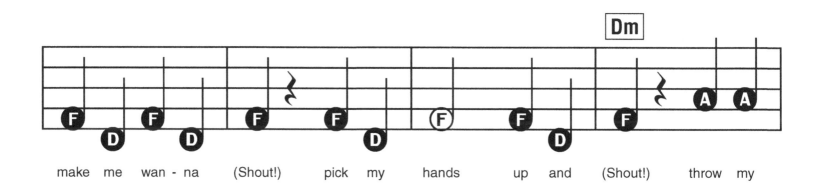

make me wan - na (Shout!) pick my hands up and (Shout!) throw my

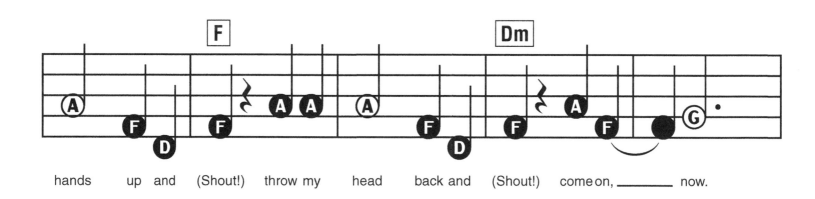

hands up and (Shout!) throw my head back and (Shout!) come on, _____ now.

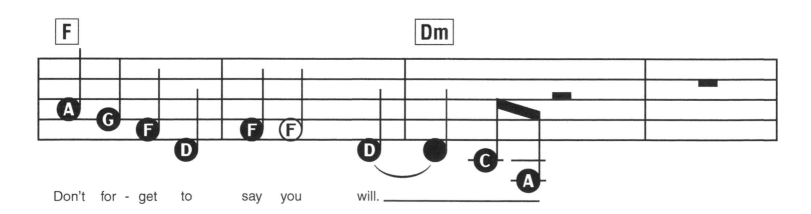

Don't for - get to say you will. _____

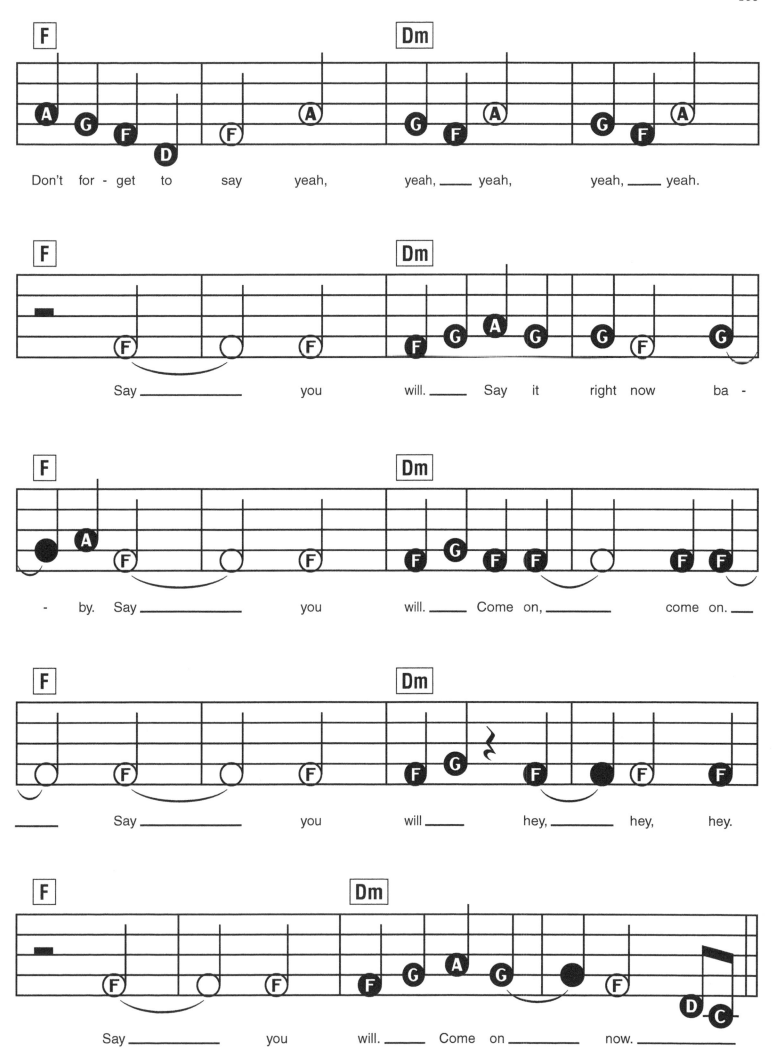

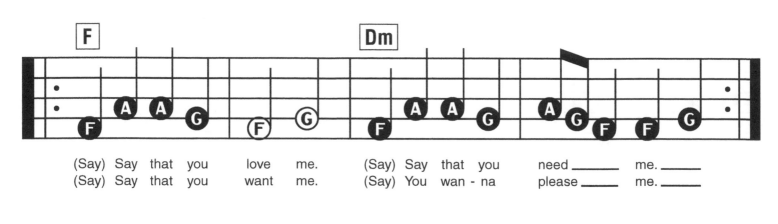

(Say) Say that you love me. (Say) Say that you need _____ me. _____
(Say) Say that you want me. (Say) You wan - na please _____ me. _____

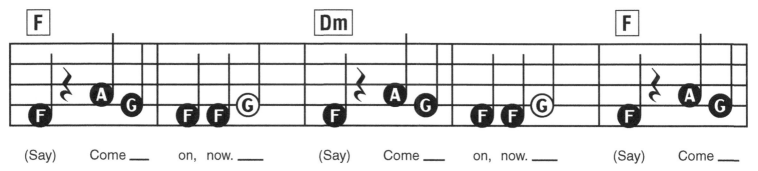

(Say) Come ___ on, now. ___ (Say) Come ___ on, now. ___ (Say) Come ___

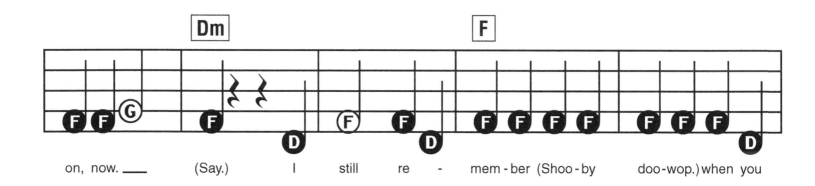

on, now. ___ (Say.) I still re - mem - ber (Shoo - by doo-wop.) when you

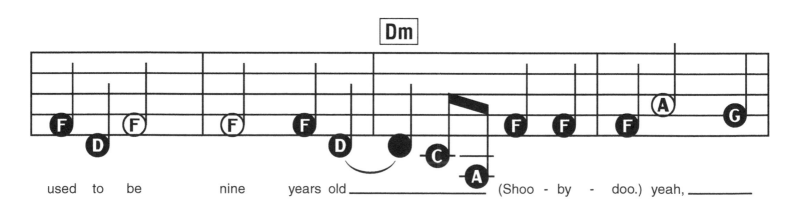

used to be nine years old _____ (Shoo - by - doo.) yeah, _____

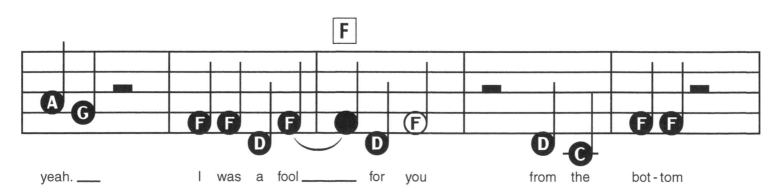

yeah. ___ I was a fool _____ for you from the bot - tom

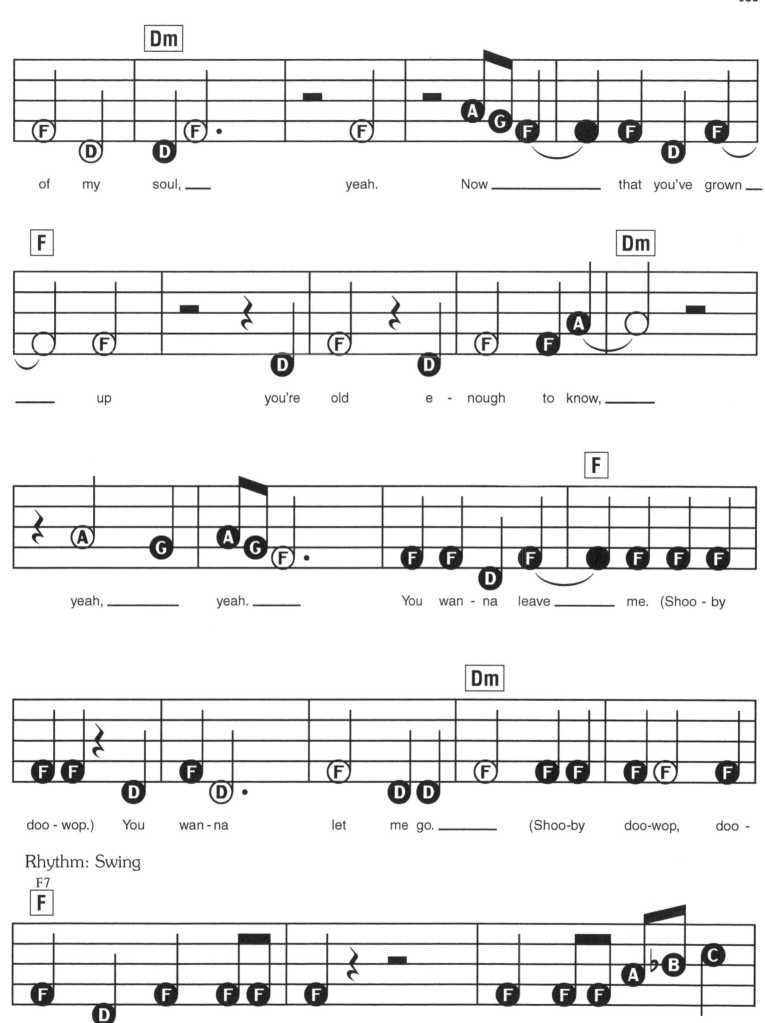

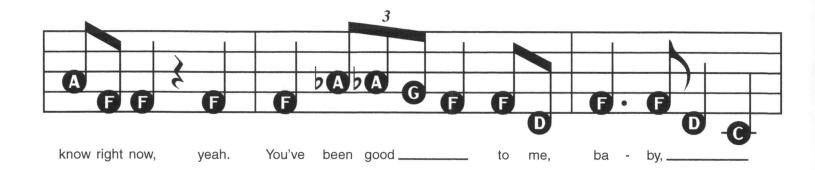

know right now,   yeah.   You've been good _____ to me, ba - by, _____

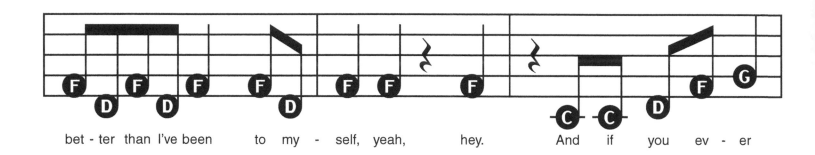

bet - ter than I've been   to my - self, yeah,   hey.   And if you ev - er

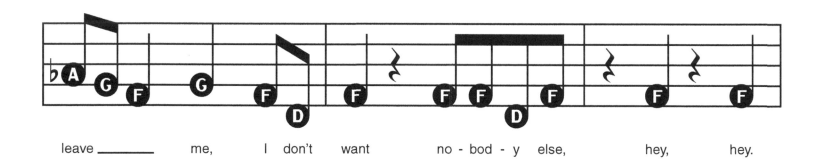

leave _____ me, I don't want no - bod - y else,   hey,   hey.

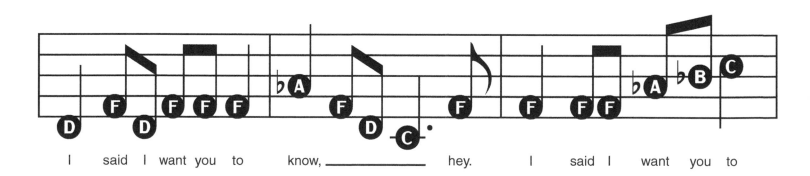

I said I want you to   know, _____ hey.   I said I want you to

Rhythm: Dance or Rock   **F**

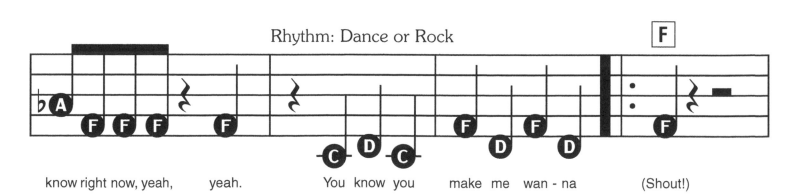

know right now, yeah,   yeah.   You know you   make me wan - na   (Shout!)

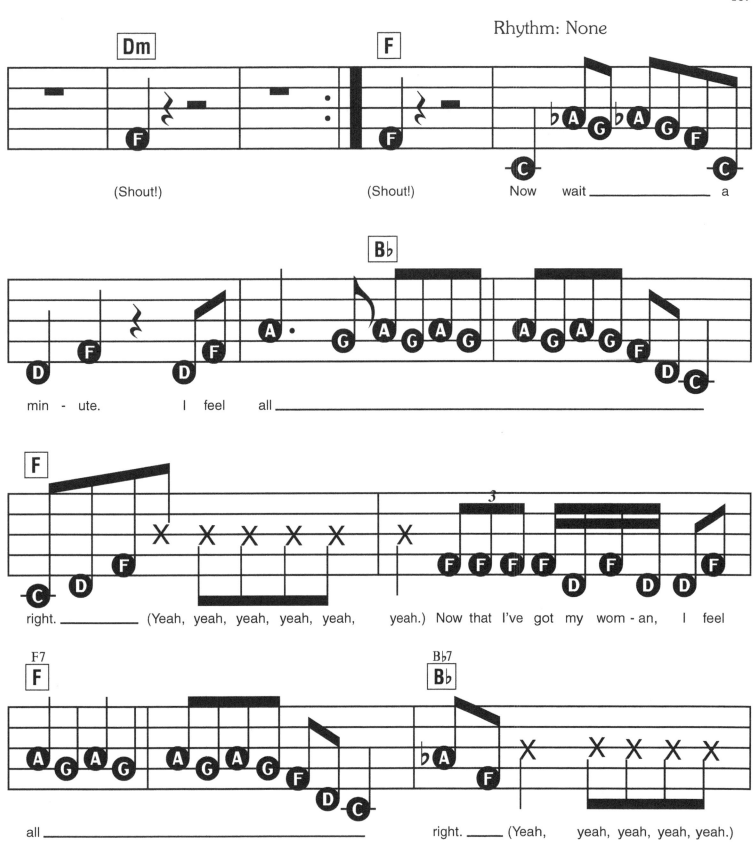

Rhythm: None

(Shout!) (Shout!) Now wait _____ a

min - ute. I feel all _____

right. _____ (Yeah, yeah, yeah, yeah, yeah, yeah.) Now that I've got my wom - an, I feel

all _____ right. ____ (Yeah, yeah, yeah, yeah, yeah.)

Rhythm: Dance or Rock

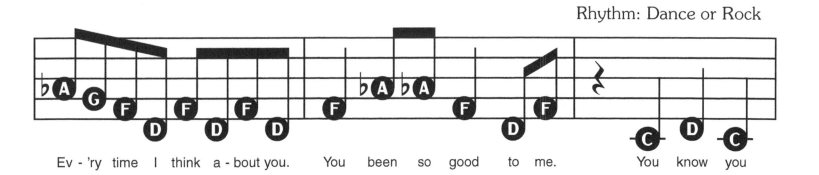

Ev - 'ry time I think a - bout you. You been so good to me. You know you

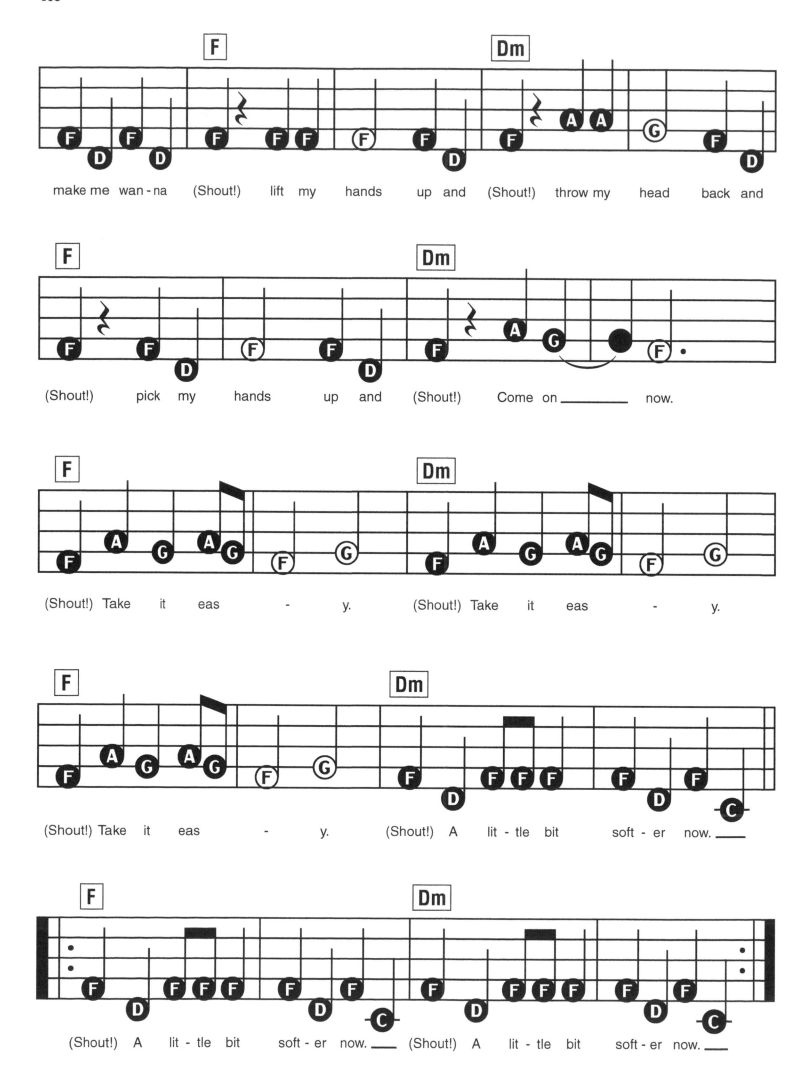

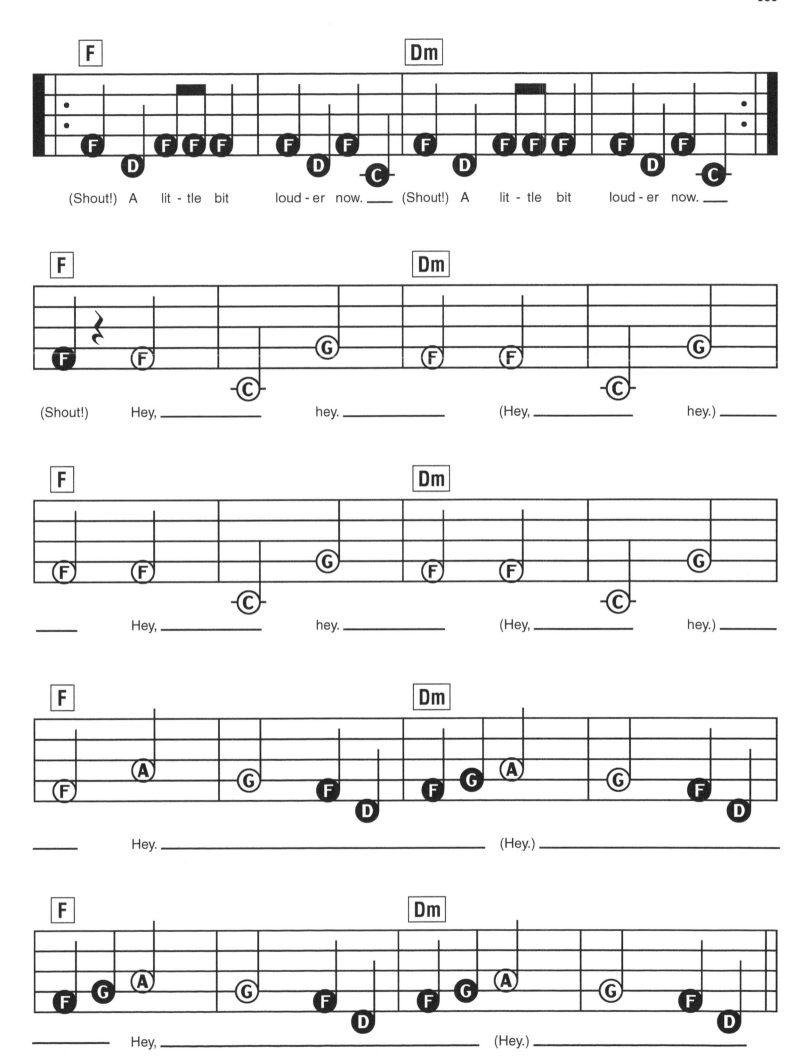

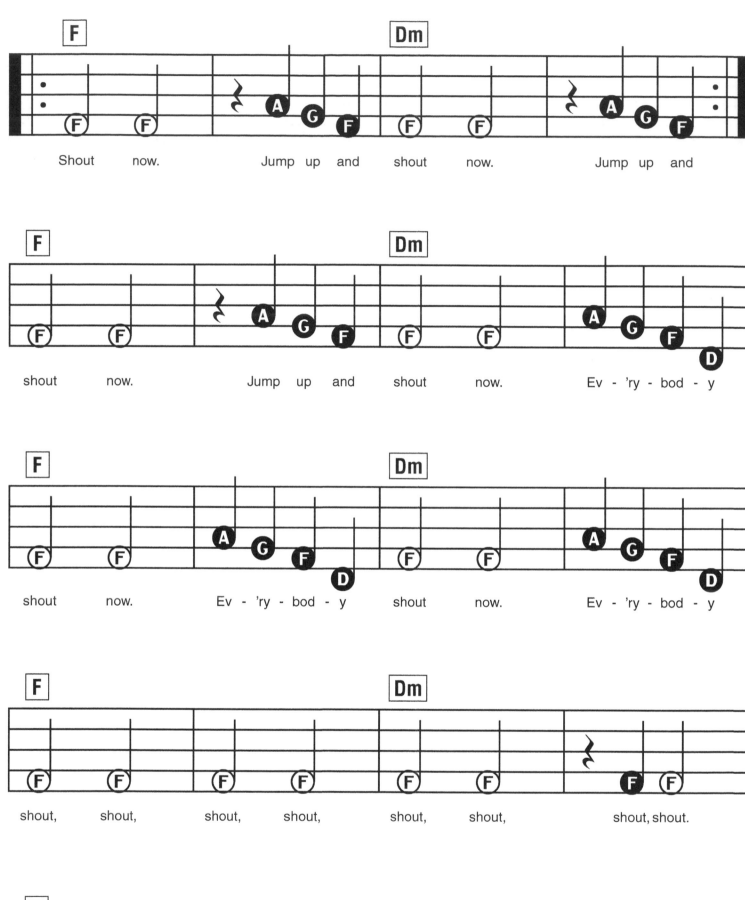

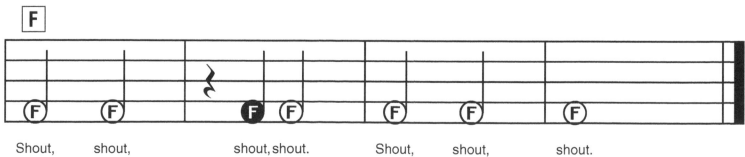

Soul Man

Registration 9
Rhythm: 8 Beat or Rock

Words and Music by Isaac Hayes
and David Porter

Com - in'   to you   on   a
got
brought up   on   the
a

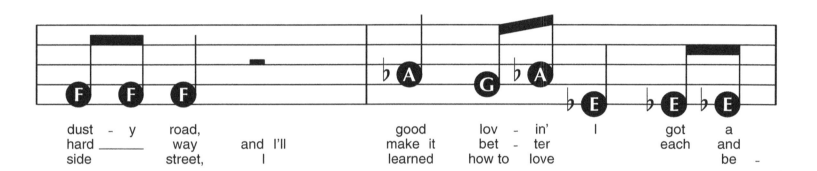

dust - y road,   and I'll   good   lov - in'   I   got   a
hard   way   make it   bet - ter   each   and
side   street,   I   learned how to love   be -

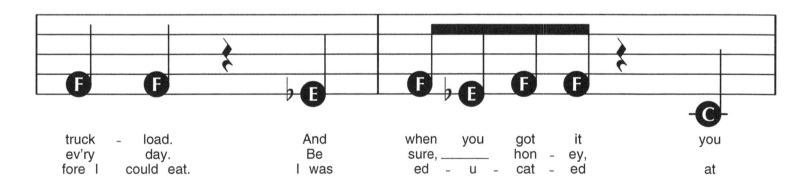

truck - load.   And   when you got it   you
ev'ry   day.   Be   sure,   hon - ey,
fore I could eat.   I was   ed - u - cat - ed   at

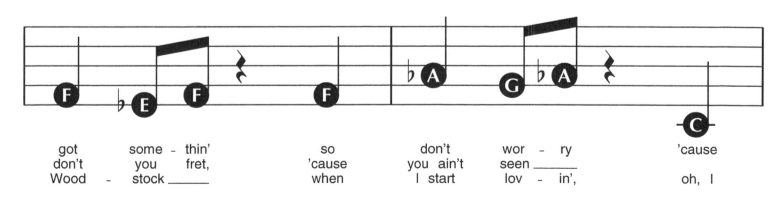

got some - thin'   so   don't wor - ry   'cause
don't you fret,   'cause   you ain't seen
Wood - stock   when   I start lov - in',   oh, I

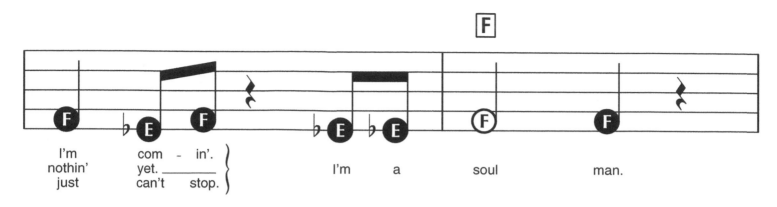

I'm   com - in'.
nothin'   yet. _____
just   can't   stop.

I'm   a   soul   man.

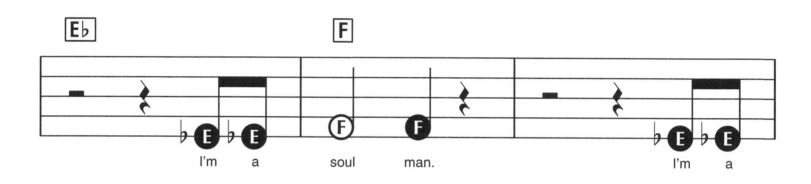

I'm   a   soul   man.   I'm   a

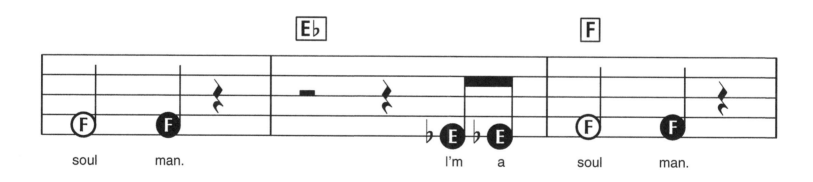

soul   man.   I'm   a   soul   man.

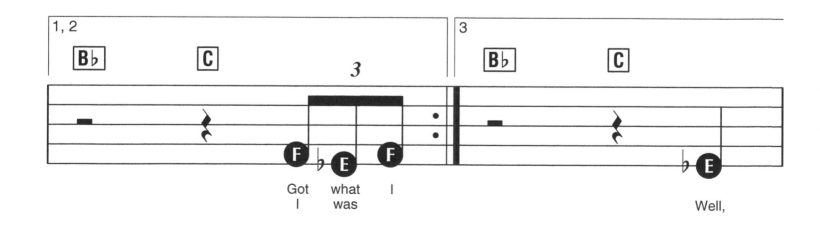

I   Got   what   I   was   Well,

113

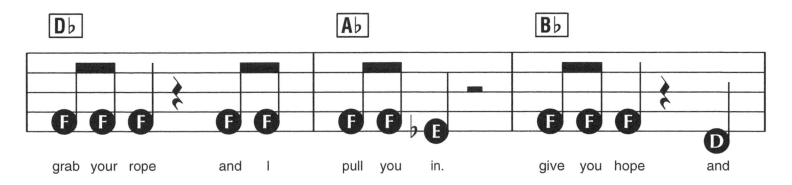

grab your rope and I pull you in. give you hope and

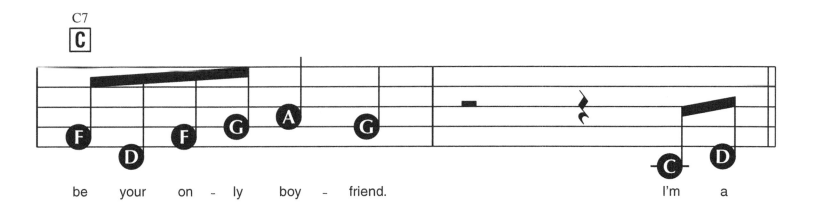

be your on – ly boy – friend. I'm a

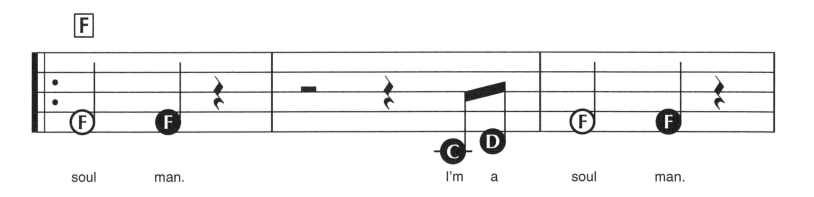

soul man. I'm a soul man.

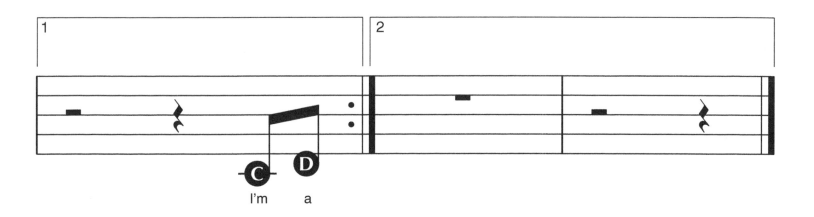

I'm a

Super Freak

Registration 2
Rhythm: Rock

Words and Music by Rick James
and Alonzo Miller

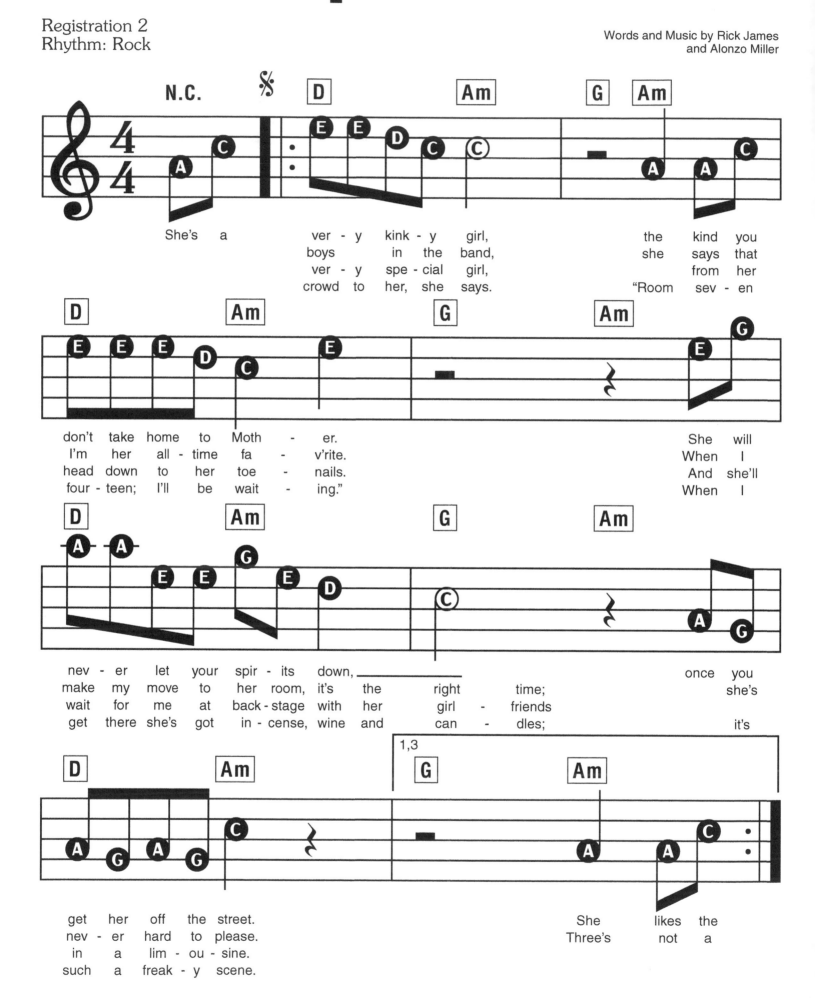

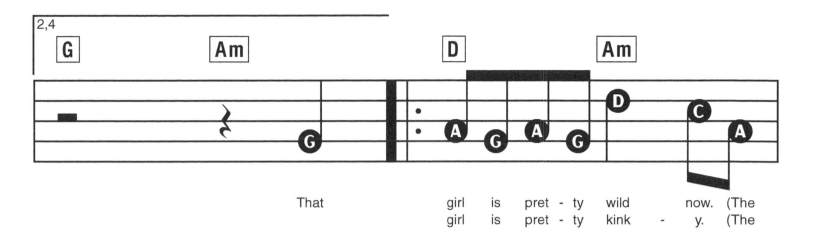
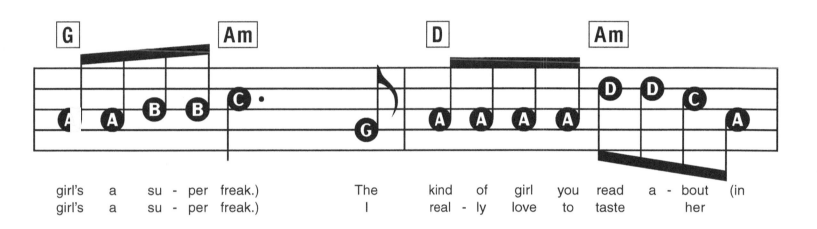
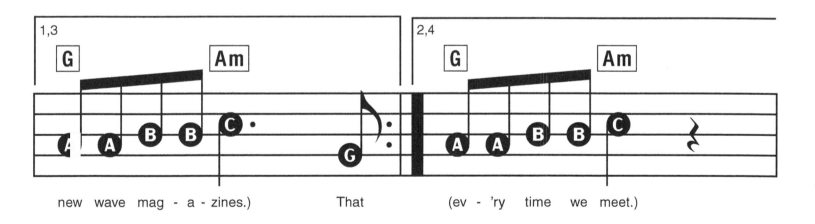
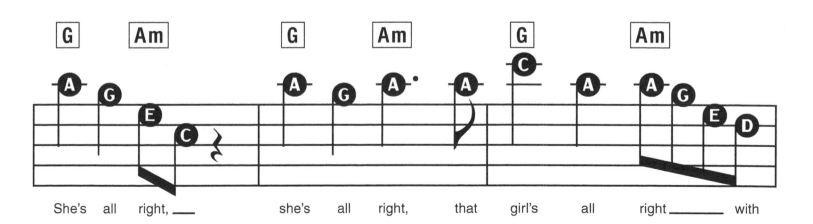

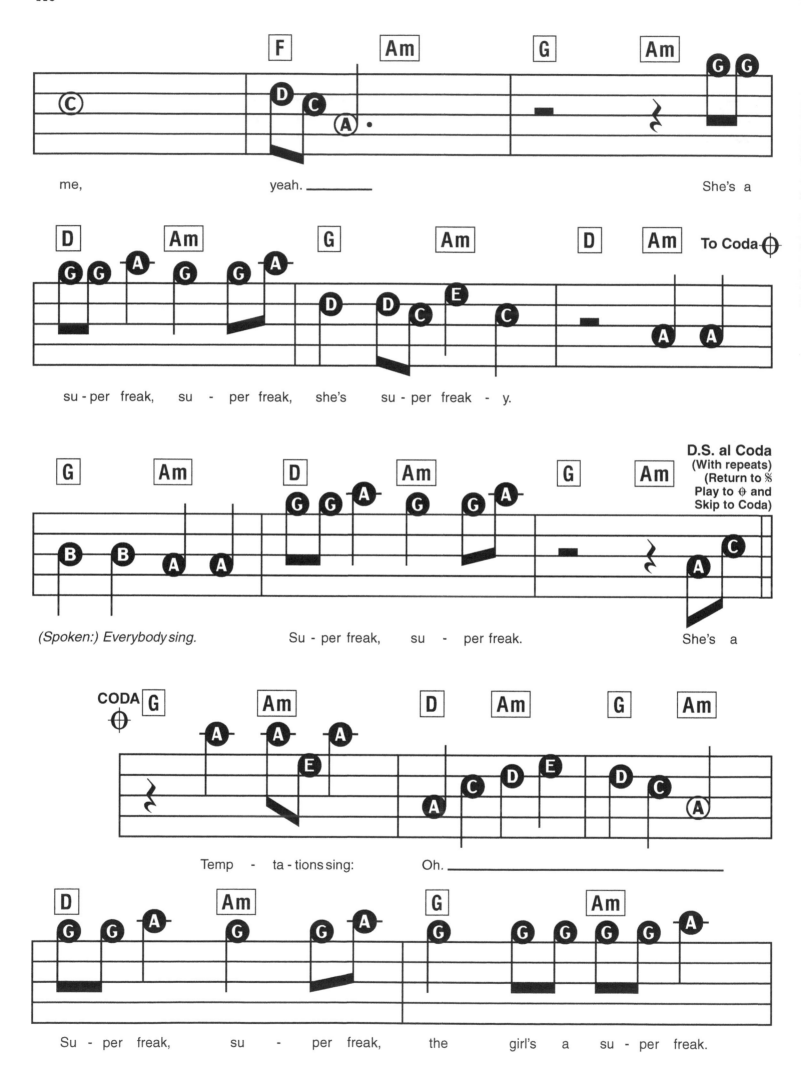

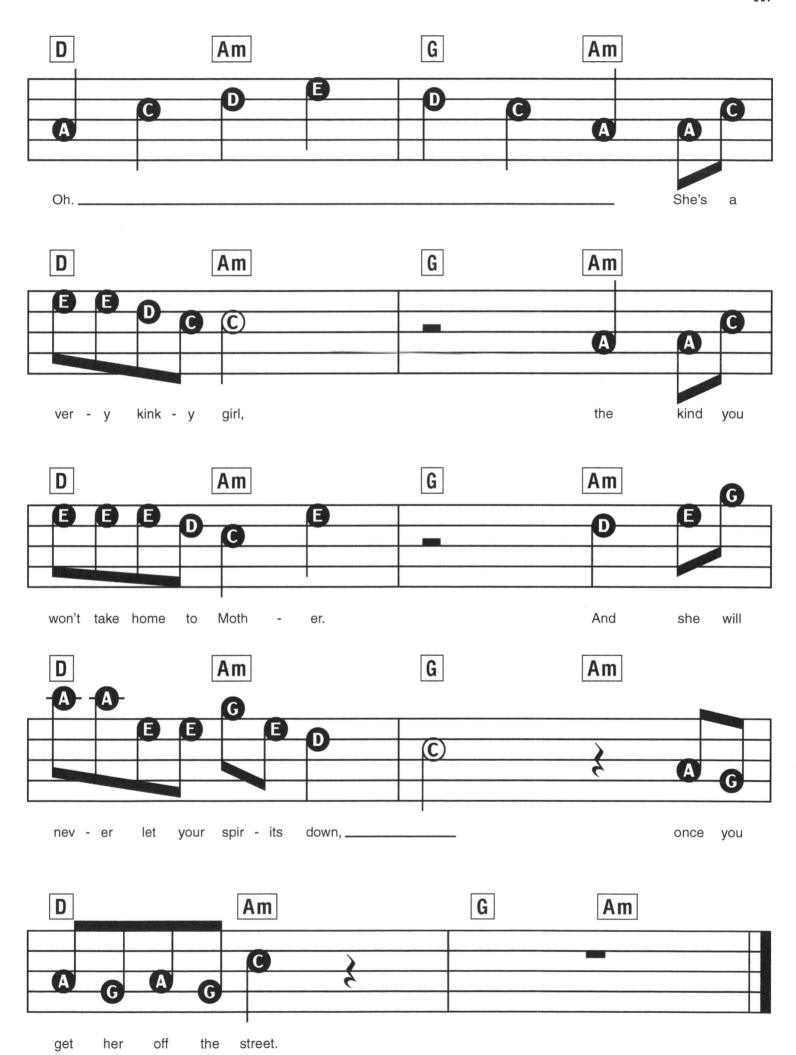

Tequila

Registration 8
Rhythm: Latin Rock or Rock

By Chuck Rio

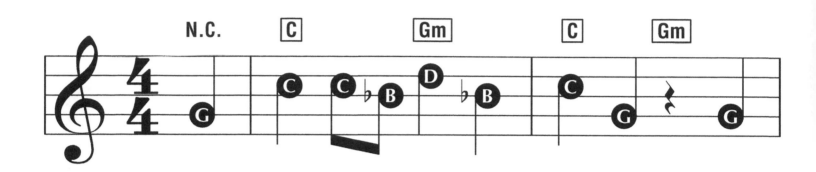

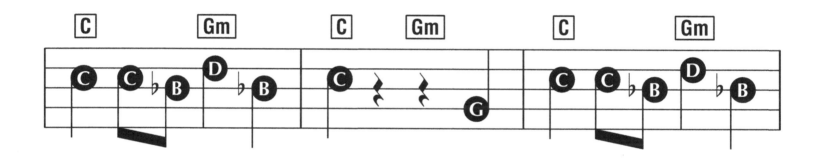

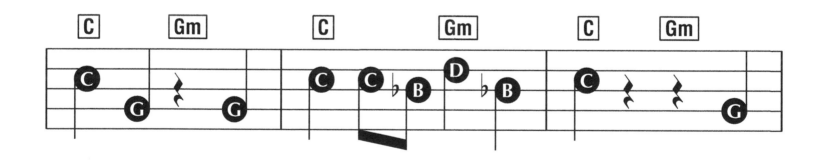

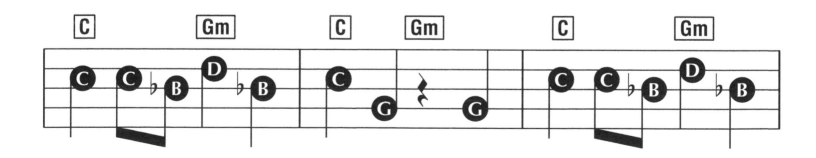

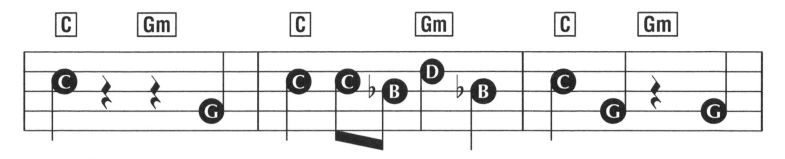

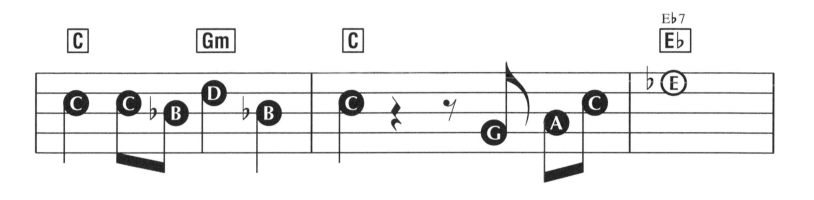

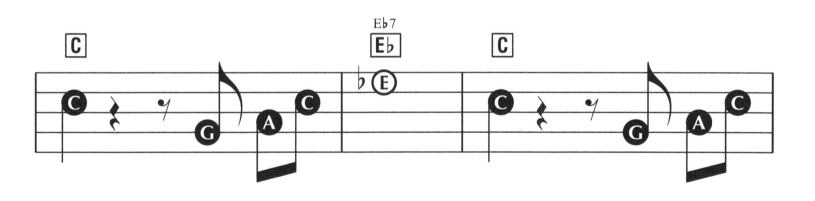

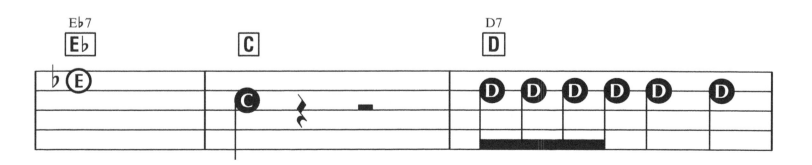

120

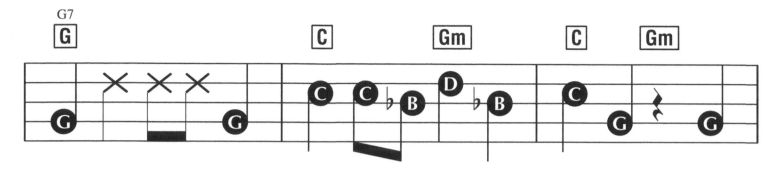

(Spoken:) Te - qui - la!

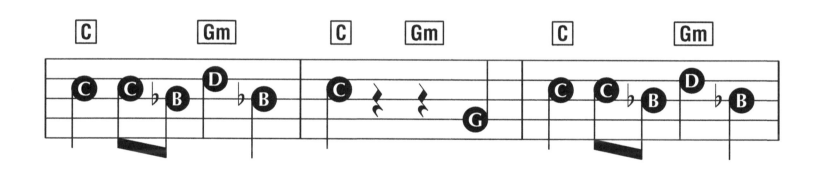

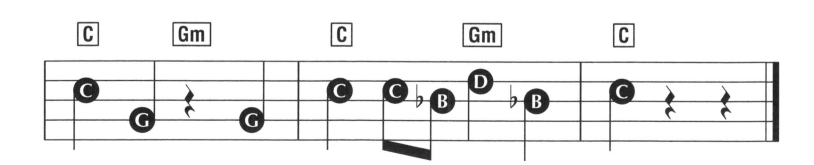

Twist and Shout

Registration 4
Rhythm: Rock

Words and Music by Bert Russell
and Phil Medley

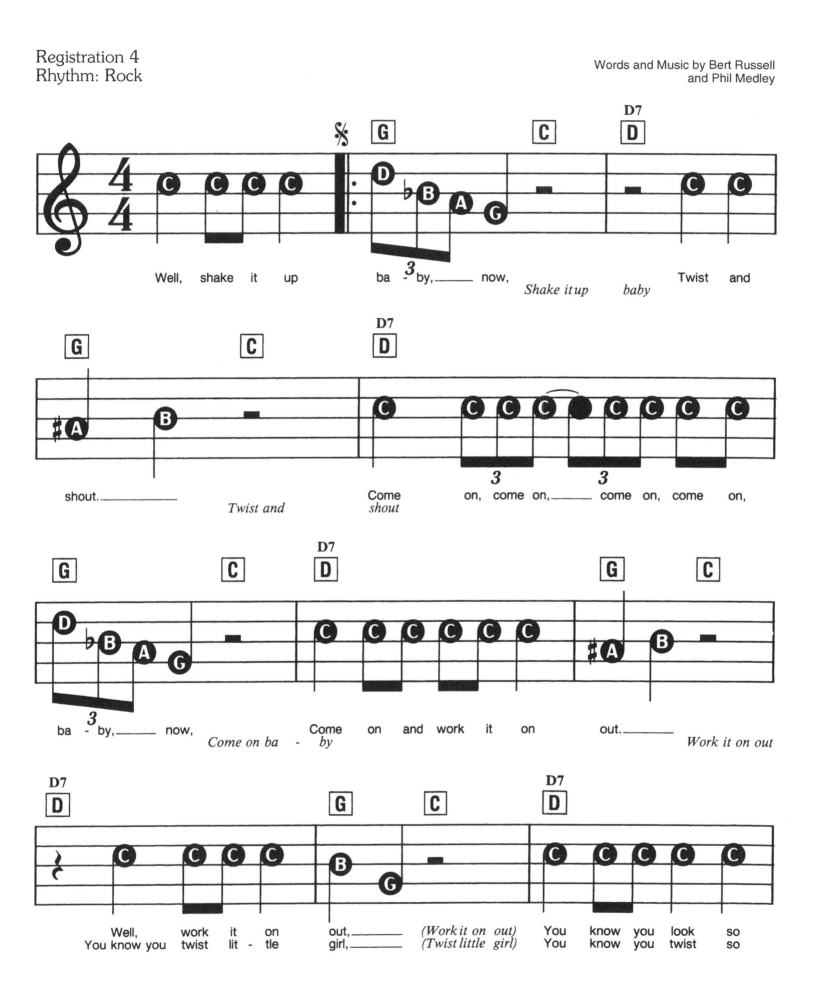

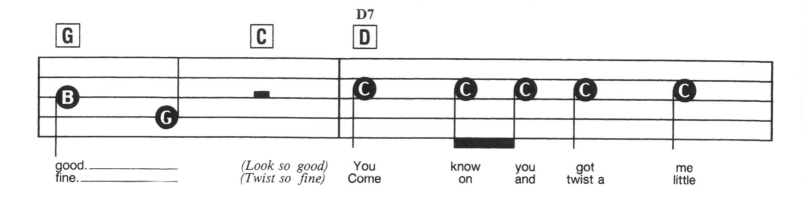

good._____
fine._____
(Look so good)
(Twist so fine)
You Come know on you and got twist a me little

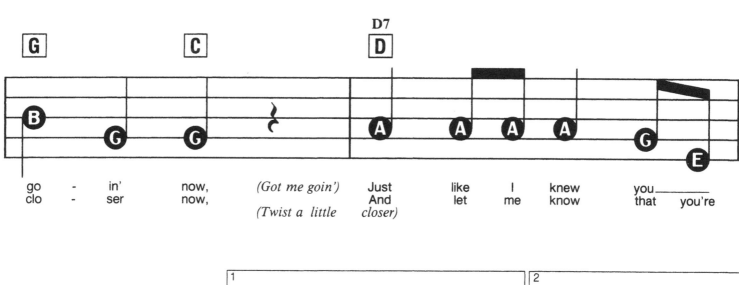

go - in' now,
clo - ser now,
(Got me goin')
(Twist a little closer)
Just And like let I me knew know you that you're

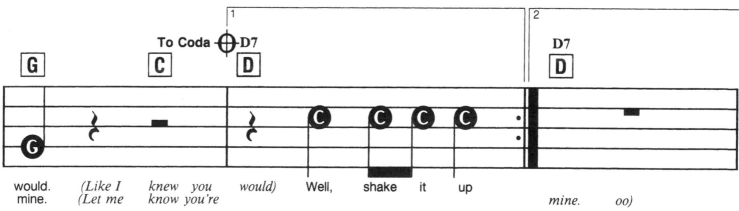

would.
mine.
(Like I knew you would)
(Let me know you're
Well, shake it up mine. oo)

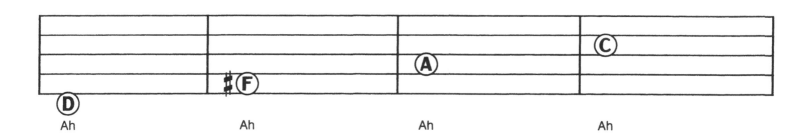

Ah   Ah   Ah   Ah

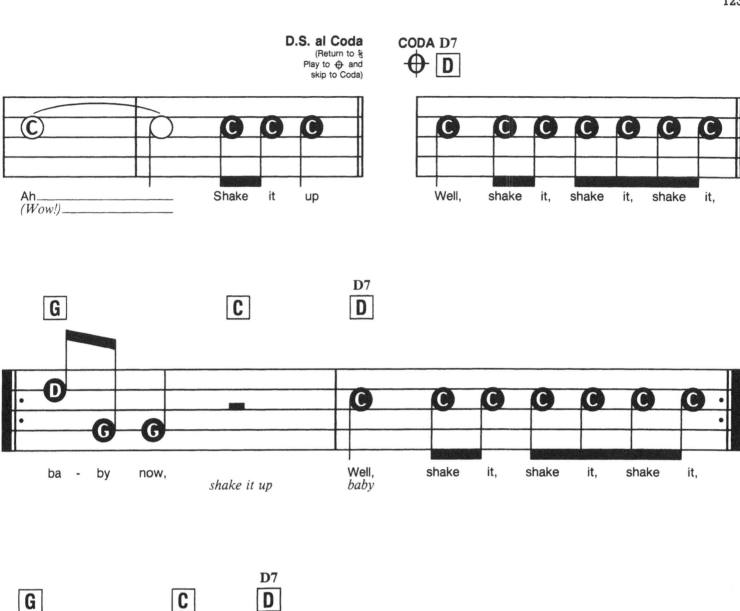

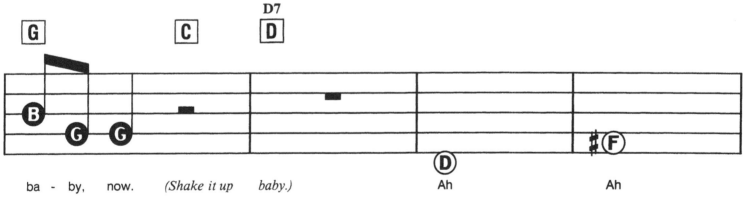

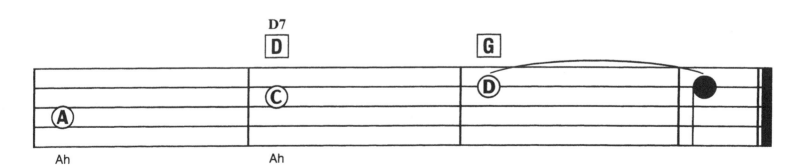

The Twist

Registration 5
Rhythm: Rock

Words and Music by
Hank Ballard

Come on ba - by, _____ let's do _____ the twist.

Come on ba - by, _____ let's do the

twist. Take me by my lit - tle hand, _____

_____ and go like this. Ee oh,

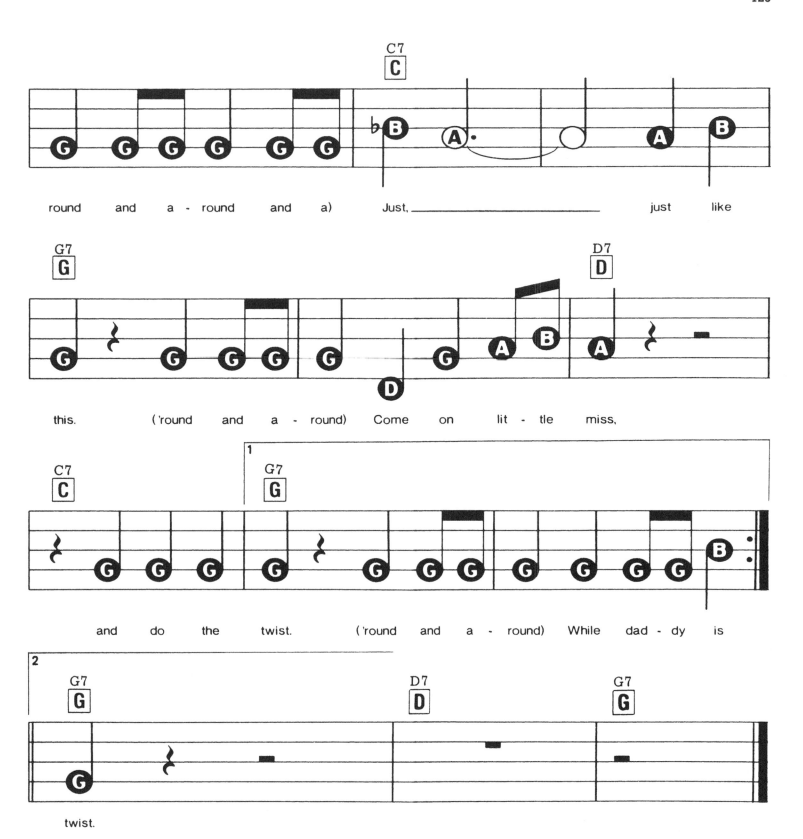

Verse 2
While daddy is sleeping and mama ain't around,
While daddy is sleeping and mama ain't around,
We're gonna twisty, twisty, twisty until we tear the house down.

You should see my little sis,
You should see my little sis,
She knows how to rock and she knows how to twist.

Walking on Sunshine

Registration 1
Rhythm: 8 Beat or Rock

Words and Music by
Kimberley Rew

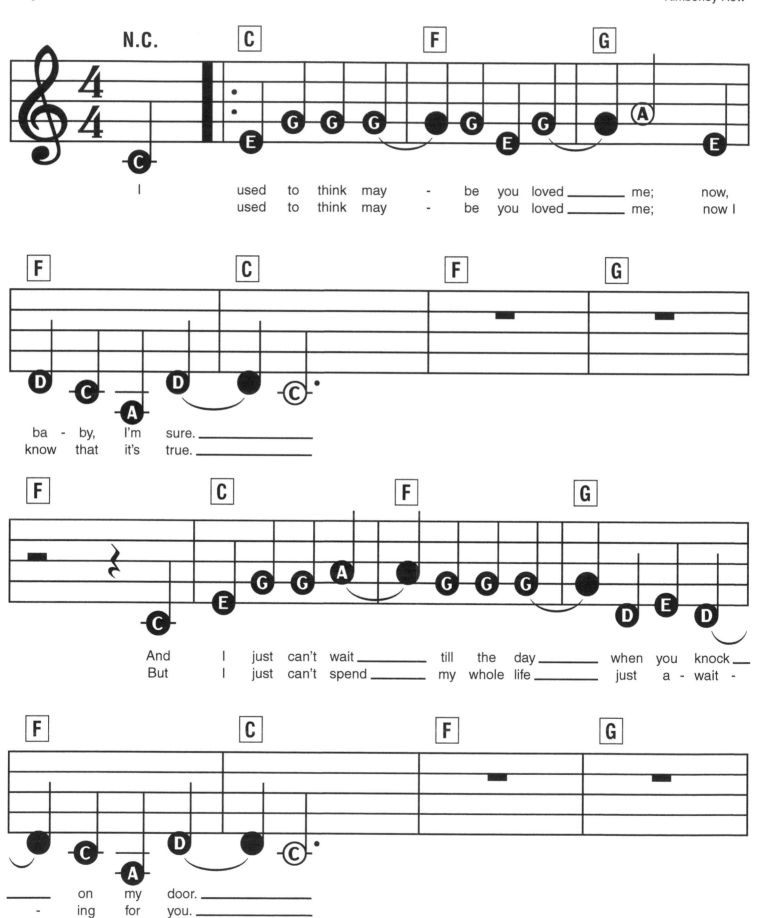

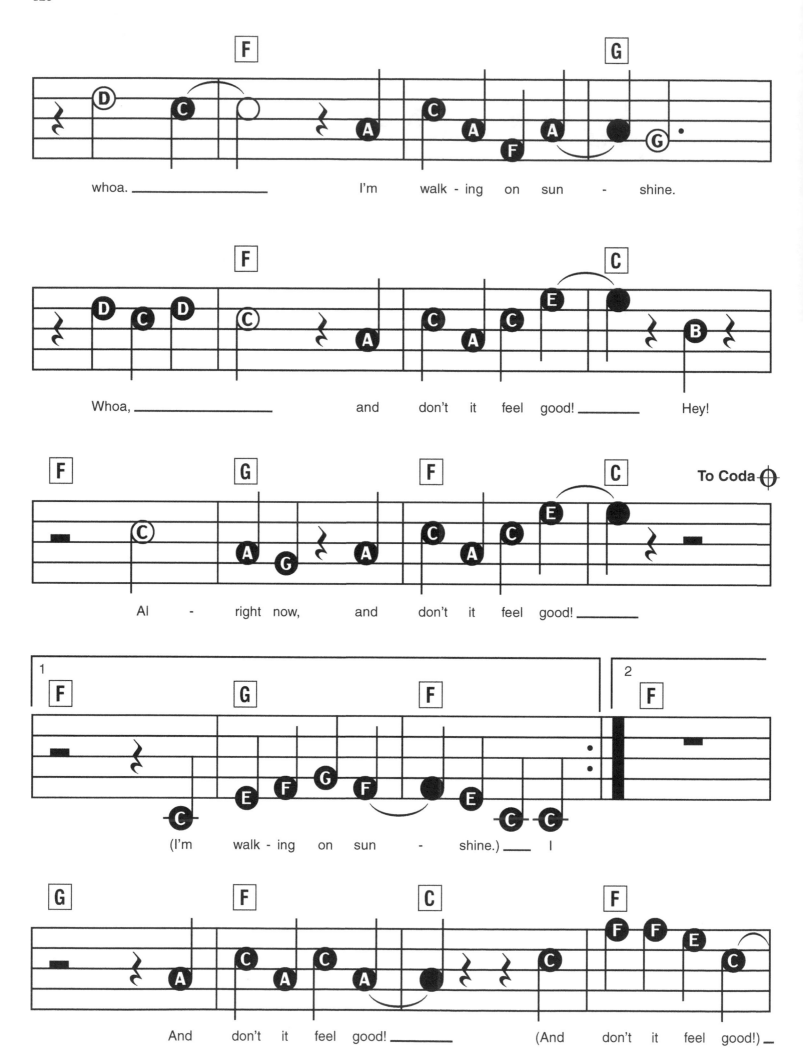

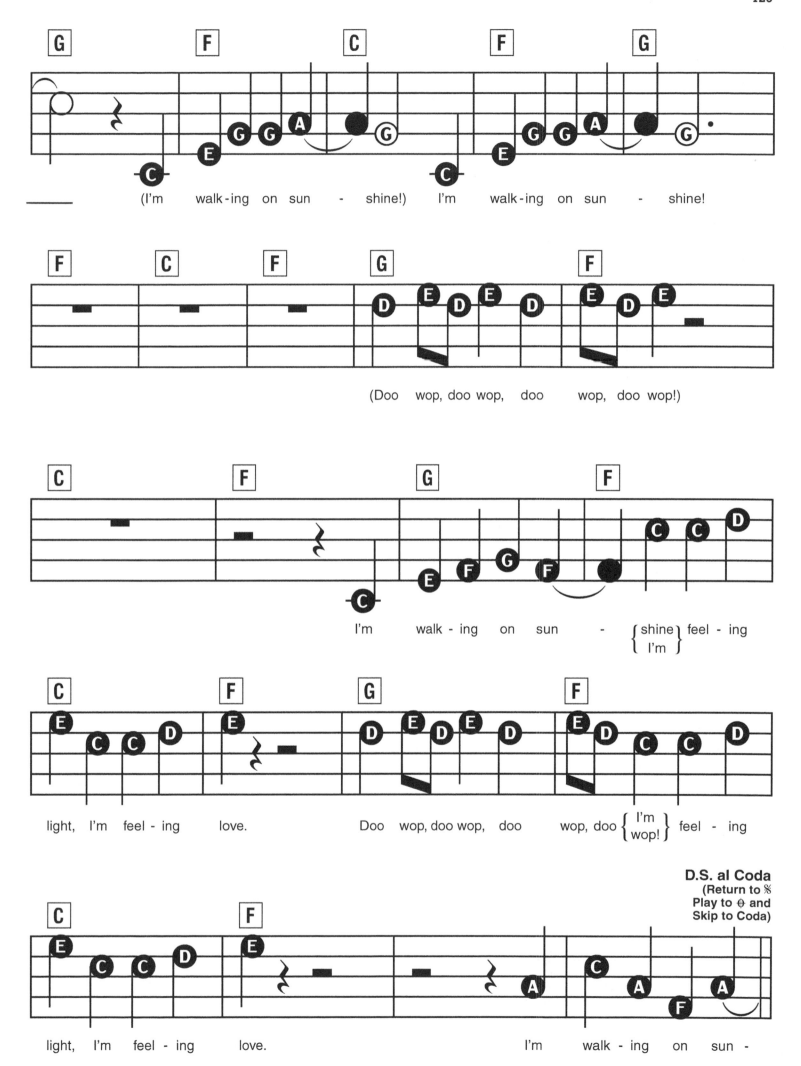

(I'm walk-ing on sun - shine!) I'm walk-ing on sun - shine!

(Doo wop, doo wop, doo wop, doo wop!)

I'm walk - ing on sun - {shine / I'm} feel - ing

light, I'm feel - ing love. Doo wop, doo wop, doo wop, doo {I'm / wop!} feel - ing

D.S. al Coda
(Return to ⅋
Play to ⊕ and
Skip to Coda)

light, I'm feel - ing love. I'm walk - ing on sun -

130

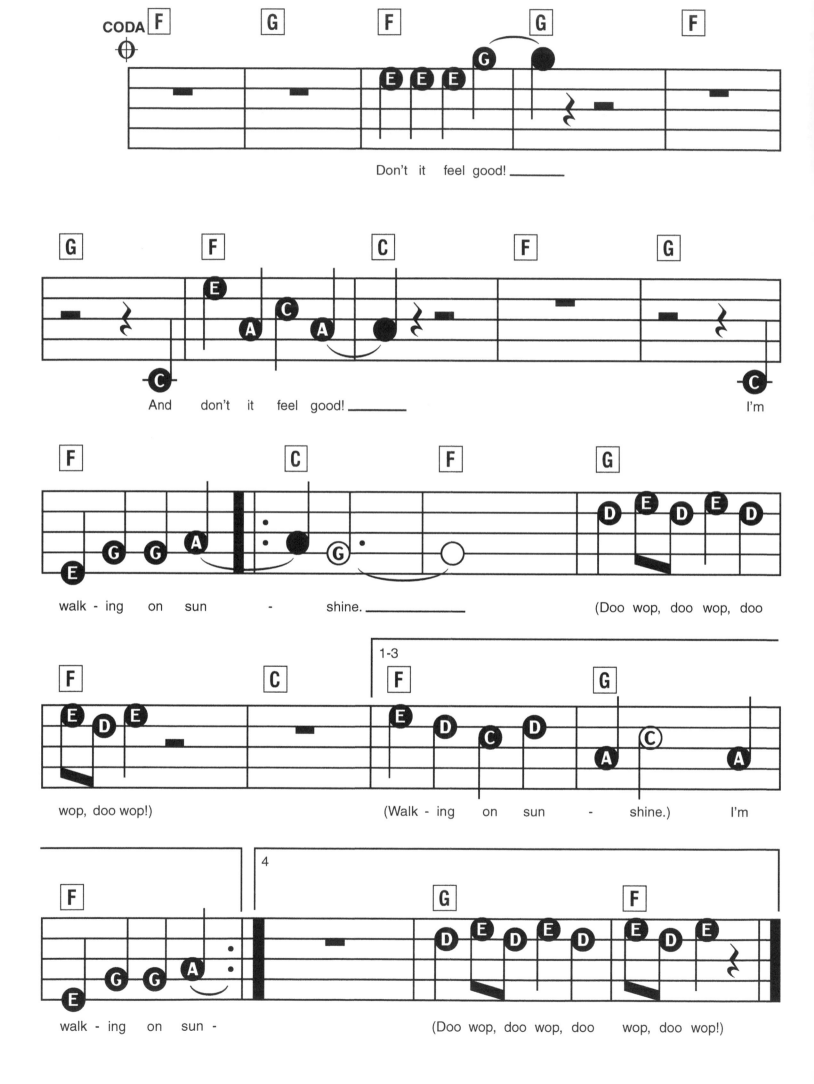

We're Not Gonna Take It

Registration 4
Rhythm: Rock or Dance

Words and Music by
Daniel Dee Snider

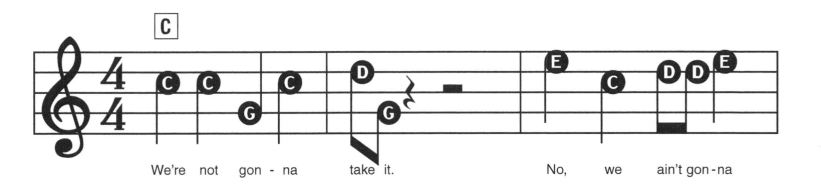

We're not gon - na take it. No, we ain't gon -na

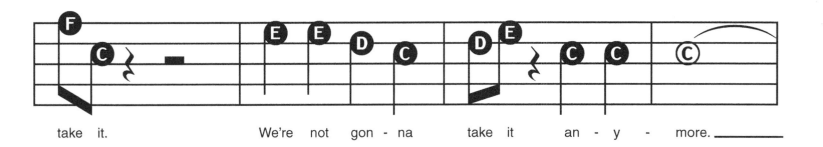

take it. We're not gon - na take it an - y - more. _____

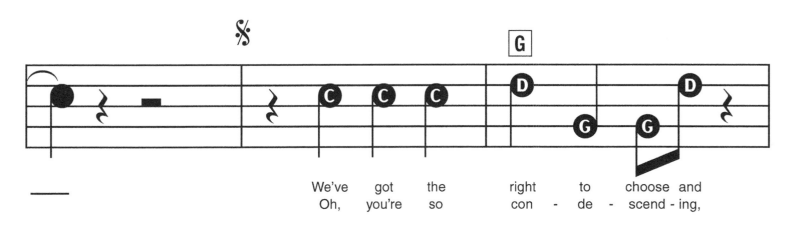

We've got the right to choose and
Oh, you're so con - de - scend - ing,

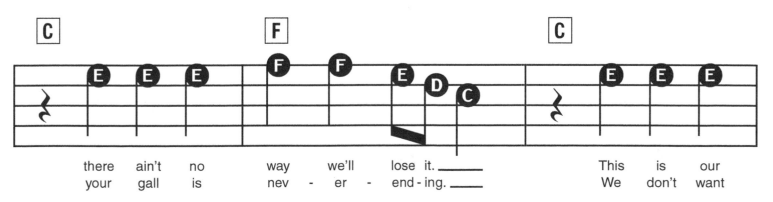

there ain't no way we'll lose it. _____ This is our
your gall is nev - er - end -ing. _____ We don't want

132

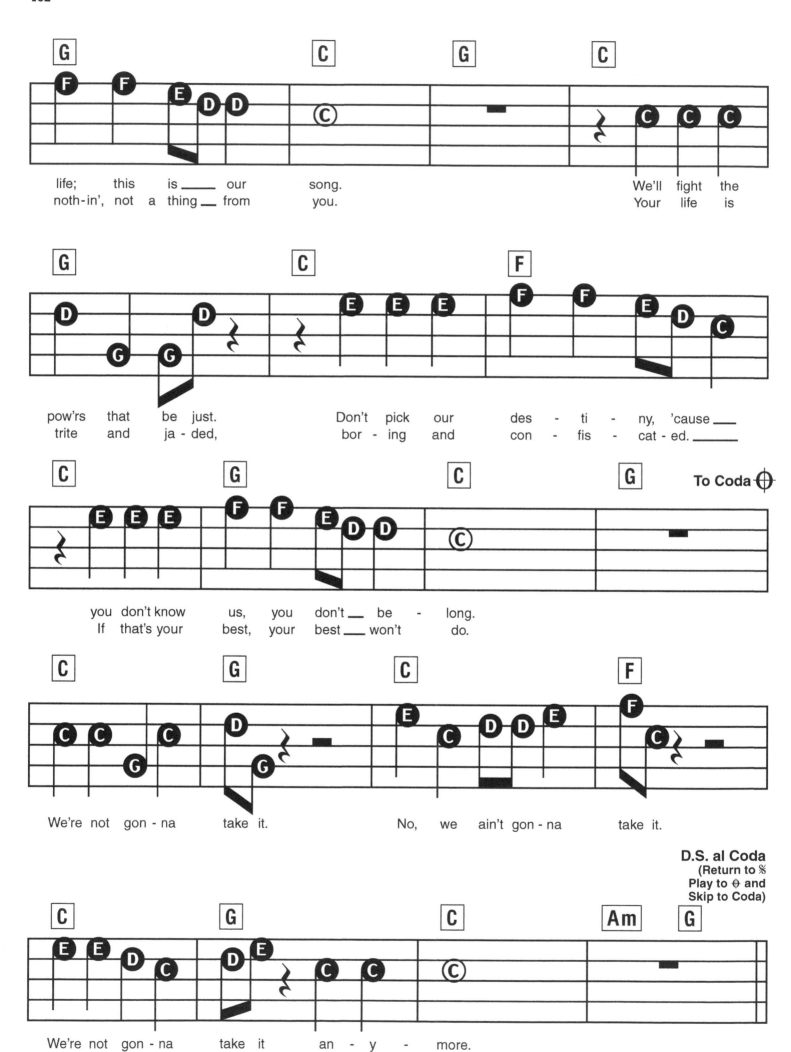

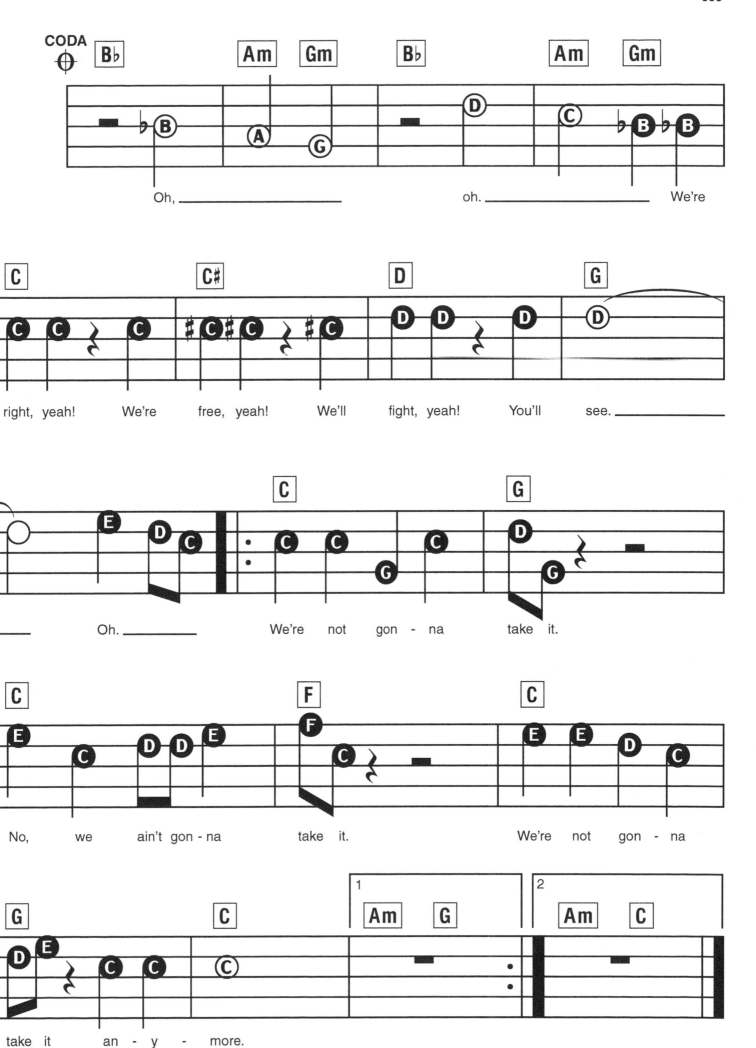

My Sharona

Registration 4
Rhythm: Rock

Words and Music by Doug Fieger
and Berton Averre

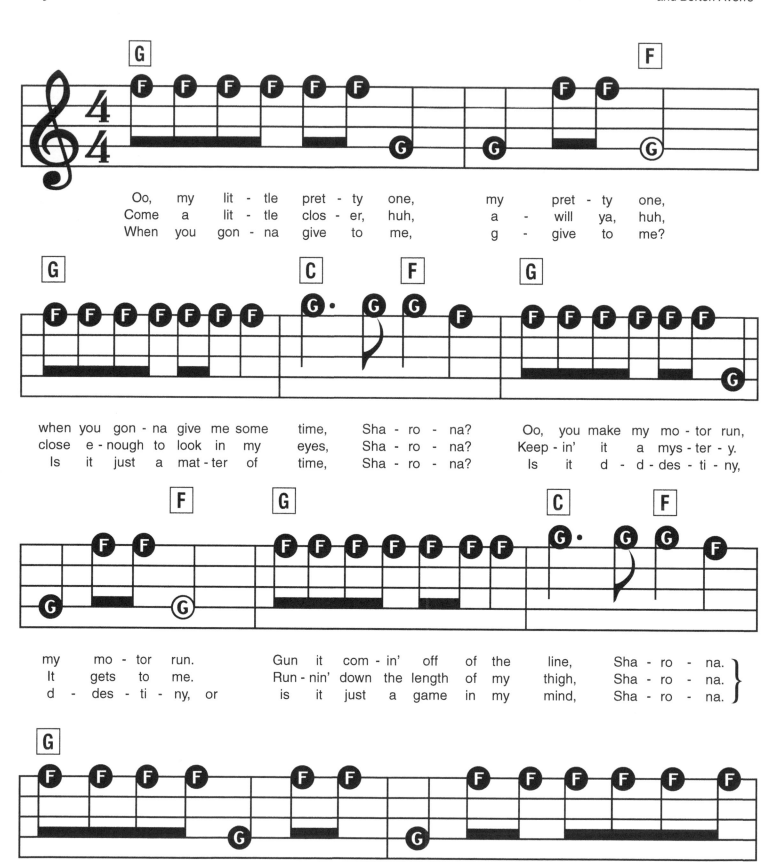

Oo, my lit - tle pret - ty one, my pret - ty one,
Come a lit - tle clos - er, huh, a - will ya, huh,
When you gon - na give to me, g - give to me?

when you gon - na give me some time, Sha - ro - na? Oo, you make my mo - tor run.
close e - nough to look in my eyes, Sha - ro - na? Keep - in' it a mys - ter - y.
Is it just a mat - ter of time, Sha - ro - na? Is it d - d - des - ti - ny,

my mo - tor run. Gun it com - in' off of the line, Sha - ro - na.
It gets to me. Run - nin' down the length of my thigh, Sha - ro - na.
d - des - ti - ny, or is it just a game in my mind, Sha - ro - na.

Nev - er gon - na stop; give it up. Such a dirt - y mind. I

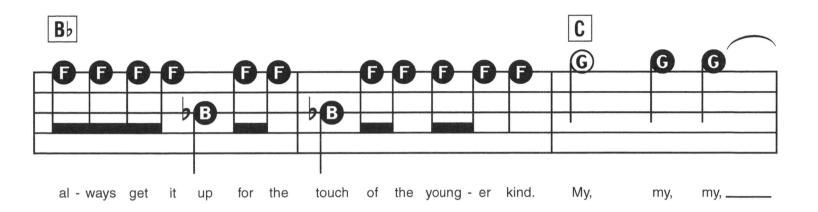

al - ways get it up for the touch of the young - er kind. My, my, my, _____

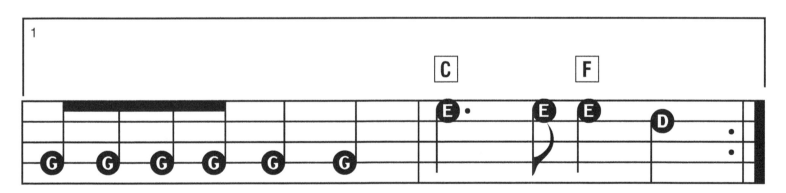

_____ yi, yi, whoo! *(Instrumental)* M - m - m - my Sha - ro - na.

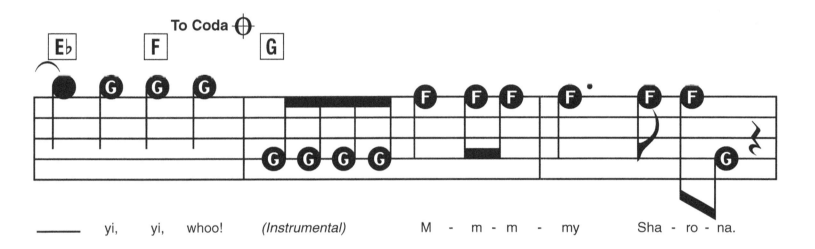

(Instrumental)

D.C. al Coda
(Return to beginning
Play to ⊕ and
Skip to Coda)

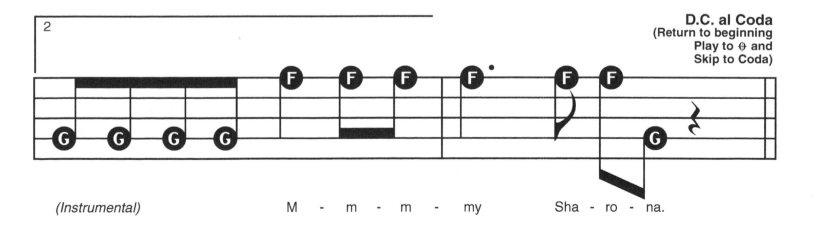

(Instrumental) M - m - m - my Sha - ro - na.

136

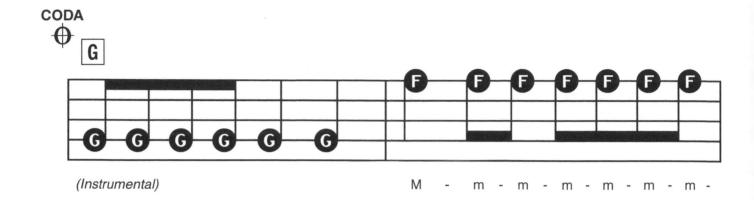

CODA

G

(Instrumental)

M - m - m - m - m - m - m -

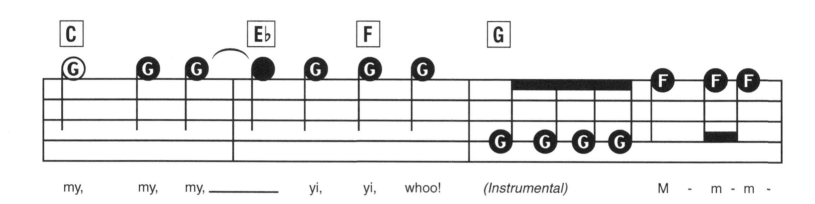

C   **E♭**   **F**   **G**

my,   my,   my, _____   yi,   yi,   whoo!   (Instrumental)   M - m - m -

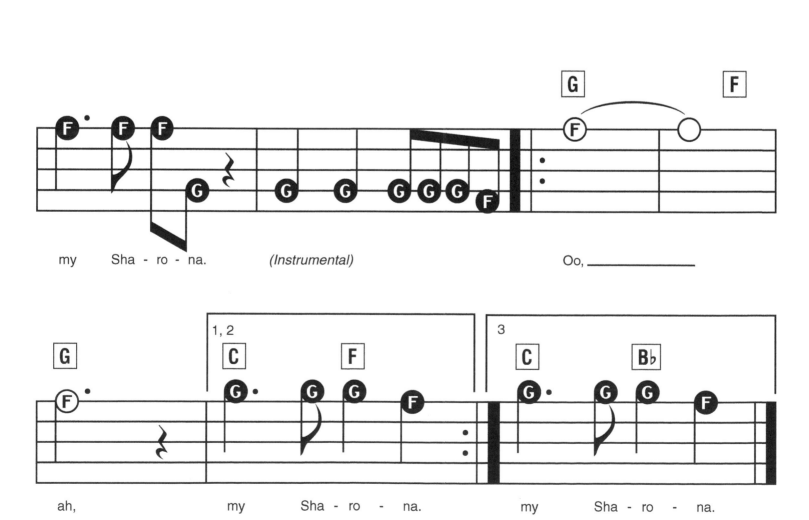

G   **F**

my   Sha - ro - na.   (Instrumental)   Oo, _____

G   1, 2   **C**   **F**   3   **C**   **B♭**

ah,   my   Sha - ro - na.   my   Sha - ro - na.

What I Like About You

Registration 4
Rhythm: Rock

Words and Music by Michael Skill,
Wally Palamarchuk and James Marinos

What I like a-bout you,
you, you hold me tight.
you keep me warm at night.

Tell me I'm the on - ly one,
Nev - er wan - na let you go,

wan - na come o - ver to - night. Yeah!
know you make me feel al - right. Yeah!

Keep on whis-per-ing in my ear, tell me all the things that

Y.M.C.A.

Registration 9
Rhythm: Disco

Words and Music by Jacques Morali,
Henri Belolo and Victor Willis

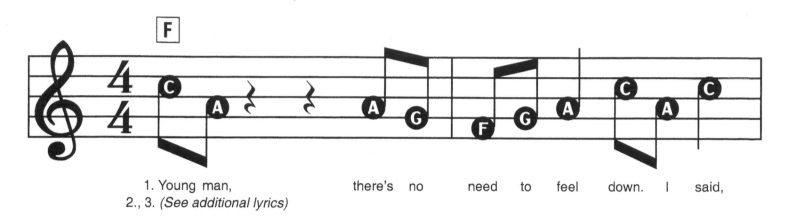

1. Young man, there's no need to feel down. I said,
2., 3. *(See additional lyrics)*

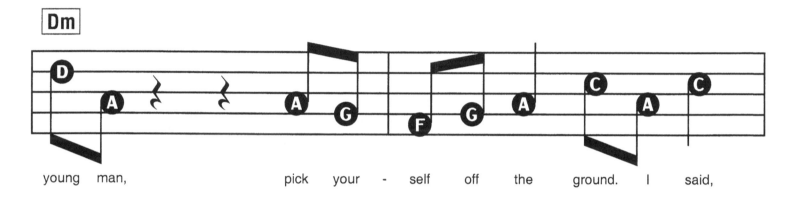

young man, pick your - self off the ground. I said,

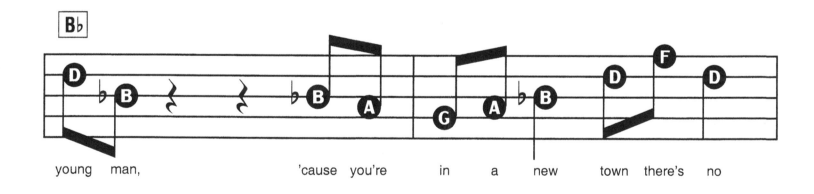

young man, 'cause you're in a new town there's no

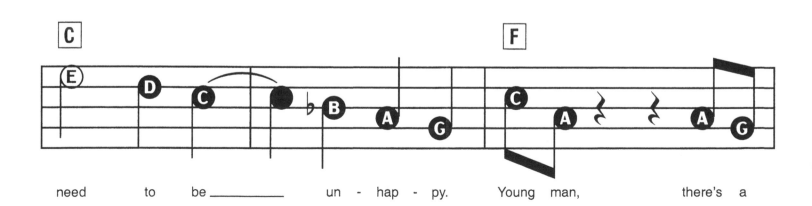

need to be _____ un - hap - py. Young man, there's a

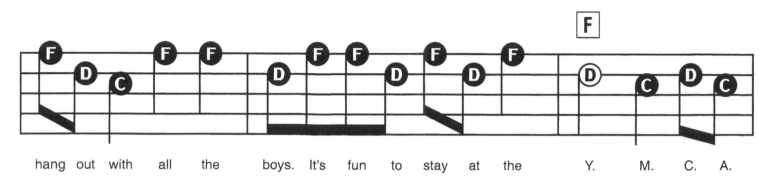

hang out with all the boys. It's fun to stay at the Y. M. C. A.

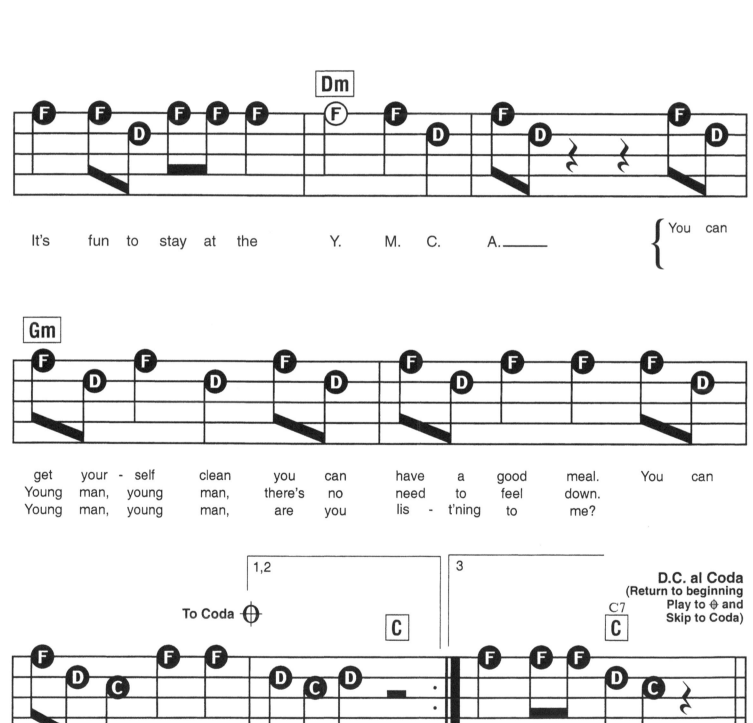

It's fun to stay at the Y. M. C. A._____ { You can

get your - self clean you can have a good meal. You can
Young man, young man, there's no need to feel down.
Young man, young man, are you lis - t'ning to me?

1,2

To Coda ⊕

C

3

D.C. al Coda
(Return to beginning
Play to ⊕ and
Skip to Coda)

C7

C

do what - ev - er you feel._____
Young man, young man, pick your-
Young man, young man, what do

self off the ground.____

CODA

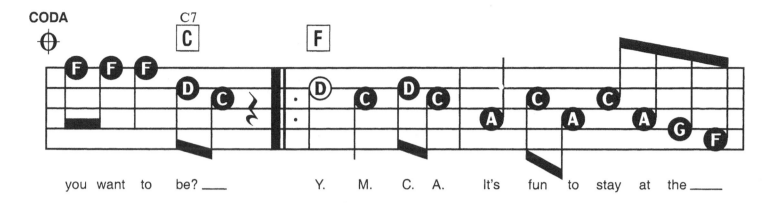

you want to be? ___   Y. M. C. A.   It's fun to stay at the ___

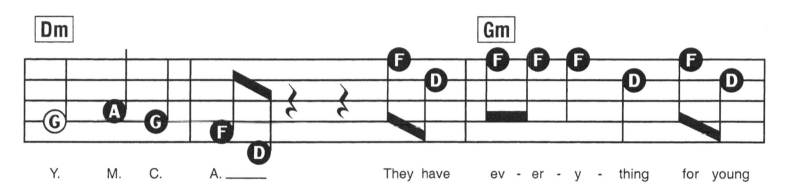

Y. M. C. A. ___   They have ev - er - y - thing for young

Repeat and Fade

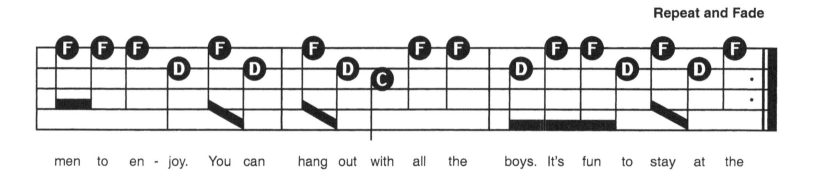

men to en - joy. You can hang out with all the boys. It's fun to stay at the

Additional Lyrics

2. Young man, are you listening to me?
I said, young man what do you want to be?
I said, young man you can make real your dreams
But you've got to know this one thing.

No man does it all by himself.
I said, young man put your pride on the shelf.
And just go there to the Y.M.C.A.
I'm sure they can help you today.
Chorus

3. Young man, I was once in your shoes
I said, I was down and out and with the blues.
I felt no man cared if I were alive.
I felt the whole world was so jive.

That's when someone came up to me
And said, "Young man, take a walk up the street.
It's a place there called the Y.M.C.A.
They can start you back on your way."
Chorus

 **Registration Guide**

• Match the Registration number on the song to the corresponding numbered category below. Select and activate an instrumental sound available on your instrument.

• Choose an automatic rhythm appropriate to the mood and style of the song. (Consult your Owner's Guide for proper operation of automatic rhythm features.)

• Adjust the tempo and volume controls to comfortable settings.

Registration

1	Mellow	Flutes, Clarinet, Oboe, Flugel Horn, Trombone, French Horn, Organ Flutes
2	Ensemble	Brass Section, Sax Section, Wind Ensemble, Full Organ, Theater Organ
3	Strings	Violin, Viola, Cello, Fiddle, String Ensemble, Pizzicato, Organ Strings
4	Guitars	Acoustic/Electric Guitars, Banjo, Mandolin, Dulcimer, Ukulele, Hawaiian Guitar
5	Mallets	Vibraphone, Marimba, Xylophone, Steel Drums, Bells, Celesta, Chimes
6	Liturgical	Pipe Organ, Hand Bells, Vocal Ensemble, Choir, Organ Flutes
7	Bright	Saxophones, Trumpet, Mute Trumpet, Synth Leads, Jazz/Gospel Organs
8	Piano	Piano, Electric Piano, Honky Tonk Piano, Harpsichord, Clavi
9	Novelty	Melodic Percussion, Wah Trumpet, Synth, Whistle, Kazoo, Perc. Organ
10	Bellows	Accordion, French Accordion, Mussette, Harmonica, Pump Organ, Bagpipes